How to Eva a Franchise

How to Evaluate a Franchise

Dedicated to my family
Phyllis, Paul, Sarah, David, Susan, Rafi, Adina, Daniel,
Tamar, Sophie, Avi and Jenna.

Published by
Franchise World
Highlands House, 165 The Broadway, London SW19 1NE.
Tel. 020 8605 2555   Fax. 020 8605 2556
www.franchiseworld.co.uk   info@franchiseworld.co.uk

© Martin Mendelsohn 2007

ISBN 0-9551938-1-8

First published 1980
Ninth edition 2007

Printed and bound in Great Britain

How to Evaluate a Franchise

MARTIN MENDELSOHN

Author

Dr. Martin Mendelsohn
Chair of the Franchising Group
Eversheds

Dr. Martin Mendelsohn has been a leading figure in franchising for over 40 years. He is chair of the Franchise Group at Eversheds, one of the country's leading legal firms. He is also visiting professor of franchising at Middlesex University Business School, London, where he has assisted with the introduction of undergraduate and masters courses in franchising in which he lectures.

Mendelsohn has advised governments about franchising, under the aegis of OECD, ILO, UNDP and the UK Know How Fund.

He is the author of *Franchising Law*, *The Guide to Franchising*, *How to Franchise Your Business*, *How to Franchise Internationally*, *How to Buy a Franchise*, the bfa guide *The Ethics of Franchising*, and editor of the bi-monthly publication *The Journal of International Franchising Law*, *Franchising in Europe* and the *International Encyclopaedia of Franchising* Law and co-author of *A Guide to the EC Block Exemption Regulation for Vertical Agreements* and *Negotiating an International Master Franchise Agreement*. His books have been published in 15 languages, including Chinese and Russian, and are in demand worldwide.

He also writes regularly in *Franchise World*, Britain's leading franchise news magazine, as well as other publications around the world. He is also in demand in many parts of the world as a speaker at franchise seminars, conventions and exhibitions.

The UK's leading franchise practice*
Ensuring the foundations of your business

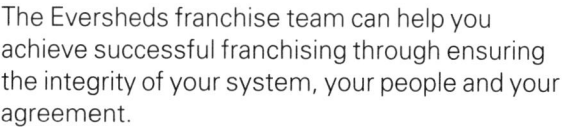

The Eversheds franchise team can help you achieve successful franchising through ensuring the integrity of your system, your people and your agreement.

Leading the team, **Chris Wormald** and **Martin Mendelsohn**, are the only lawyers in the UK and Europe ranked in the top 10 'Most Highly Regarded Individuals', a global survey carried out by Who's Who Legal, the research partner of the International Bar Association, in 2006.

Contact them on 0845 497 4862 or chriswormald@eversheds.com

www.eversheds.com

© EVERSHEDS LLP 2006.
Eversheds LLP is a limited liability partnership.

* Legal 500 and Chambers 2007

CONTENTS

How to Evaluate a Franchise

Foreword
By Simon Clarke

1. Franchising - what is it? 1
2. How to recognise pyramid selling 6
3. How a franchise differs from other types of business 9
4. Assessing your suitability to become a franchisee 14
5. Weighing up the advantages and disadvantages 23
6. Essential steps in assessing your franchisor 33
7. Assessing your franchisor's business proposition 40
8. The franchise agreement 47
9. Raising the finance to buy your franchise 55
10. Summing-up 59

Appendix A *British Franchise Association Code of Ethics* 61

How to Evaluate a Franchise

Foreword

by Simon Clarke FCCA

Technical and Finance Director
TaxAssist Accountants Network

Starting your own business is undoubtedly one of the most exciting things you can do, but rather than being an event it is best to think of it as a process that starts with an idea and extends beyond the first day of trading as you face ever changing opportunities and threats in your business in the early years.

You have already made an important discovery on the road to your new business. Starting as a franchisee of a (BFA) recognised franchise statistically means that you are more likely to be successful.

The franchisor will have a tried and tested system to add to your hard work and determination. You should spend lots of time evaluating the system you intend to buy into, and make sure that the franchisor allows you to contact its existing franchise network. These will be the best placed to give you an honest assessment of where the business has been and, more importantly, where it's going.

You should speak to all of the major banks, and ask them searching questions of the franchise you are interested in. You should take a copy of the franchisors accounts from Companies House and visit its head office and meet the personnel. After all, you are after a long successful relationship and you deserve to make sure that you are entirely happy.

We know that for most business owners, this is a passion and not just a work schedule, so the most important thing to remember is to enjoy yourself. I wish you a successful new start.

CHAPTER ONE
Franchising - what is it?

FRANCHISING has become a very popular term. Briefly, it is used by many business people to describe certain types of licensing arrangements. Thus, we speak of a franchise granted for the running of a television station, a franchise granted by a car manufacturer to dealers and a franchise to run a railway. Many distributorship and agency arrangements are also described as franchises. On a more popular basis, there is character merchandising in which a well-known person, or the owner of an invented character (e.g. Mickey Mouse, Buzz Lightyear, the Simpsons), grants franchises (licences) to others, entitling them to make use of a name. We even have the film industry calling the name of a film a franchise.

These arrangements are quite common. They have been with us for many years and no change has been made in these traditional relationships which would justify them now being called franchises, rather than continuing to be termed agency, distributorship or licence arrangements or whatever else they were previously called.

The more popular use of the word franchise has arisen from the development of what is called the *business format franchise*. Some also call it a *trade mark/trade name franchise*. The former name is preferred because it is so descriptive. It is the *business format franchise* with which this particular booklet is concerned.

- **The business format franchise is the grant of a licence by one person (the franchisor) to another (the franchisee), which entitles (and usually requires) the franchisee to carry on business under the trade mark/trade name of the franchisor and in doing so to make use of an entire package (know-how), comprising all the elements necessary to**

1

establish a person previously untrained and inexperienced in the conduct of a business to run the business developed by the franchisor under the brand and, after training, to run the business on a predetermined basis with continuing assistance.

These business format elements comprise:-
- The entire business concept.
- A process of initiation and training in all aspects of the running of the business, according to the concept.
- A continuing relationship with the franchisor providing assistance and guidance.

The entire business concept

This involves the development by the franchisor of a successful way of carrying on the business in all its aspects which comprises the basis of its know-how. The franchisor will develop what may be described as a blueprint for conducting the business. This blueprint should:-

1. Eliminate so far as possible the risks inherent in opening a new business. For example, the product range (or service) and all operational aspects of the business should be thoroughly market tested in pilot operations run by the franchisor. The resulting business should be identified with the brand developed by the franchisor. This ensures that the franchisee new to the business does not make the mistakes which would be made by a non-franchised new business person.

2. Enable a person, who has never before opened or operated a business, to open up in business on his own account, not only with a pre-established format, but with the backing of an organisation (i.e. the franchisor is analogous to a head office support team) which would not otherwise be available to him and at a price which that person can afford.

3. Set out in detail exactly how the business should be run.

Process of initiation and training

The franchisee must be trained in the business methods which are necessary to operate the business, according to the blueprint. This may involve training in the use of specialised equipment, marketing methods, preparation of the product, application of processes and/or delivery of services. The franchisee should be trained so that he is relatively expert in all the spheres which are necessary for the operation of the particular business. This will include, where appropriate, stock selection, staff utilisation, staff selection and training, business management techniques, accounting and reporting methods, marketing and promotion. The franchisee should also be assisted in the selection of premises (if appropriate), or the defining of a trading area (for mobile franchises) and in all the steps necessary to establish and open the business.

Continuing process of assistance and guidance

The franchisor will in many cases provide the sort of services included in the list below on a continuing basis, depending, of course, upon the particular type of business:-

- Regular visits from, and access to, field support staff of the franchisor to assist in correcting or preventing deviations from the blueprint which may cause trading difficulties for the franchisee.

- Liaison between the franchisor, the franchisee, and all other franchisees to exchange ideas and experiences.

- Product or concept innovation, including the investigation of marketability and compatibility with the existing business.

- Training and re-training facilities for the franchisee and his staff.

- General market research.

- National and local advertising and promotion.

- Bulk purchasing opportunities benefitting from the aggregate buying power of the network of franchisees.

- Management and accounting advice and services.
- Publication of a newsletter.
- Research into materials, processes and business methods.

It will be seen that the business format franchise is a comprehensive and continuing relationship in which the initial concept is always being developed. The resources available for such development are contributed by the franchisor and all franchisees, and are, therefore, much more considerable than any one individual could reasonably afford, or command.

As has been pointed out earlier, the expression *franchise* is now popularly used to describe all those transactions in which one person permits another to do something with its property rights. For example, petrol filling stations, car dealerships, the use of a sportsman's or an entertainer's name, are commonly called franchisee.

It is important to recognise what sort of franchise is being offered and it will then be clear as we shall see from later chapters what should be built into the franchise system and contract.

The word, franchising, can be used as a vehicle for abuse and indeed it has been in the past. It is the sort of transaction which readily lends itself to fraudulent practices. Invariably, the transaction falls into two stages:- the first is the provision of pre-opening services; the second, the continuing relationship thereafter.

If the franchisor charges too much at stage one, and is not there to provide stage two, the scope for fraud is obvious. A fraud could also be committed by franchising an untried and undeveloped concept, resulting in a franchisee being charged fees for the right to conduct a business which in reality does not exist.

In addition to this sort of abuse, there is the more sinister use of the word "franchise" to describe trading schemes which are not franchises in order to attract interest to what is a fraud. It is often not recognised that the use of the word "franchise" to describe some spurious business system is in itself a fraud, resulting in unfair criticism of bona fide franchising.

The most frequently seen fraud invariably involves the distribution of a product or products for which little market exists. The "victim" will be expected to pay relatively large sums of money to secure exclusive sales rights to a territory and to purchase a stock of the products. The problem is that no-one in the territory knows of the products and invariably they are too highly priced. At best, the fraudulent operator is using capital generated from the sale of territories to establish a business when he should be using his own capital for the purpose. At worst, he will disappear with the money and leave his "victims" high and dry.

The British Franchise Association with its ethical code and accreditation and re-accreditation of members has been material in raising standards and in granting access to members who are committed to behave ethically (see p45 for more information about the bfa).

CHAPTER TWO
How to recognise pyramid selling

THE most serious frauds which have been perpetrated were described as pyramid selling, multi-level marketing schemes or network marketing. **These are not franchise schemes although they are often confused with franchises by those who seek to profit from the vulnerability of the unwary**. They are presented as foolproof and tempting methods of making easy money and they are often marketed to would be participants by presenting successful participants, who speak of their great financial success at sales meetings.

These schemes involve the sale of distributorships to purchasers who may divide and sub-divide them, and sell them on to those whom they recruit as sub-distributors. Expansion of these 'enterprises' takes place on the chain letter principle.

The ostensible objective is to build up a sales force which will sell the company's products or services from door-to door. In practice, selling the goods or services is very often difficult. The prices are usually high and there is no established market for the products, and nor is any attempt made to advertise and promote the sale of the products. Selling distributorships is much more lucrative and this becomes effectively the company's business. Indeed, the evidence in a case heard by the High Court as long ago as 1972 showed that in the scheme, which was the subject of the case, the highest sales of products by any distributor did not exceed £130 in a year, while many thousands of pounds had been spent on selling/buying the rights to participate.

Examples of features of a pyramid scheme are the offer of a percentage payment of any sum paid to the promoter of the scheme for the recruitment of another participant, or persuading such a participant to purchase the right to progress to a higher position, or level of standing, in the scheme. Other rewards could include a profit or commission on sales, the provision for payment of services or training to other participants in the scheme, or a commission on the sales made by other participants in the scheme.

These schemes were recognised by the Government as containing elements which are dishonest and, accordingly, the Fair Trading Act 1973 contains provisions which prohibit pyramid-type schemes which do not comply with regulations which have been made under the Act. Regulations were made soon after the Act was passed.

More recently the Trading Schemes Act 1996 amended the Fair Trading Act in a number of material respects and new regulations were introduced.

The new law does not apply to what are described as "single tier" arrangements. These are arrangements where the Promotor (Franchisor) contracts directly with the Participants (Franchisees) who deal with consumers. If there is an intervening layer as there would be with a Master Franchise arrangement there may be a problem. However, if all members of the System (including the Promotor/Franchisor if they carry on business in the UK) are registered for VAT the Act would not apply.

It is vitally important to be able to recognise possible involvement with a pyramid or other such schemes and obviously before signing a contract or parting with money one should take proper professional advice. But it is a matter for suspicion if one is offered or told that there will be a reward (i.e. payment, supply of cheaper products, or any other disguised benefit) for doing something totally unrelated to the sale of the basic product or service with which the scheme is purportedly involved.

For example, one may be offered a percentage payment of any sum paid to the promoter of the scheme for recruiting another participant, or for persuading such participant to purchase a higher position in the scheme. Other rewards could include a profit or commission on sales, or the provision of services or training to other participants in the scheme, or the provision of services or training to other participants in the scheme, or a commission on sales affected by other participants in the scheme.

Attendance at meetings of the nature described above should be avoided, but if one is tempted to join such a meeting **the temptation to sign up on the spot must be resisted** so that appropriate professional advice can be taken. If one is not permitted to remove the documents one should never sign and should not pursue the proposition further.

Pyramid and other such schemes have cost some unsuspecting people a great deal of money. There are many legitimate franchises in which to invest without becoming involved in pyramid or other such schemes. No legitimate franchise will do what the pyramid or other such schemes do and that is to promise rich rewards quickly and without hard work. Whatever is being franchised legitimately will offer reasonable prospects of good rewards in return for the hard work and application which is the lot of all successful self-employed business people.

CHAPTER THREE
How a franchise differs from other types of businesses

BUYING a franchise is just like buying a business, but with a difference. What is that difference? In the case of a conventional business, the seller is asked questions and he provides accounts. The buyer makes up his mind whether he would like to buy. There are "going rates" for various types of business, and after perhaps some haggling over the price a deal is struck. The buyer takes over the business and *will run it in whatever way he thinks best*, whether or not he has had previous experience of running any business.

In the case of franchising, there are a number of other very important factors to consider. As a franchisee, you will be entering into a long-term relationship with your franchisor in which you will have to rely on him to a large extent for the success of your own business. You will not be allowed to run your business in whatever way you think fit. You will have the obligation to run it precisely in accordance with your franchisor's system.

You will find that there are four primary factors present in your business which would not be there if you were trading independently outside the franchise system. These factors are:

i) the existence of your franchisor,

ii) the obligations to use its name and systems, and submit to its control,

iii) the risk of events occurring which are detrimental to your business without you being in a position to exert any influence over them (e.g. the business failure of your franchisor or actions by other franchisees which bring the business into disrepute), and

iv) the ability of your franchisor to continue to provide you with services of a standard which makes them worthwhile and valuable to the success of your business.

You can find yourself vulnerable in each of these areas and you must, therefore, be aware of these risks in order to be able to ask the right questions and make a sound judgement when you are assessing a franchisor. In this context, it is useful to review the most common causes of failure by franchisors.

1. Inadequate pilot tests

With a new concept, there is a danger that the franchisor has not pilot-tested his system sufficiently well to have proved its viability in the market place. The problem is that it is difficult to judge what represents sufficient pilot-testing. However, if there can be any general rule, it is that the testing should be for as long as is necessary for the franchisor to prove the viability of his system in a variety of locations and market conditions. One must also ensure, for example, that seasonal factors have been recognised and allowed for by the franchisor.

In reality, it can take a new franchisor two years to develop its system to the point at which it is ready to market the franchise. In assessing a franchise, one should take great care to ensure that the pilot-testing has been fully and thoroughly carried out. As interest increases in franchising, there are likely to be more franchises on offer where proper piloting has not been done. Without being able to prove that there is a fully tested and successful system, one could probably question whether, in fact, there is a franchise to sell.

2. Poor franchisee selection

It is a common tendency in the early days of a franchise for the franchisor to accept, as franchisees, people who are unsuitable. This occurs because a franchisor who has made a large investment in establishing his business can be under a great deal of financial pressure to make some quick sales, or because it has not at that stage been able to identify properly the qualities and characteristics which its franchise calls for in a franchisee. Poor selection inevitably brings problems which slow growth and divert the management resources of the franchisor away from other vital tasks.

3. The franchise may be badly structured
This can be the. result of inadequate pilot-testing, or the inability to anticipate likely problems. Structural problems lead to operational difficulties, and these in turn to financial problems and difficulties in managing a network of franchisees.

4. The undercapitalisation of the franchisor
Many franchisors fail to recognise that it can take three to five years to reach a point at which they achieve some profitability, depending on their healthy rate of growth. The franchisor will need the capital or access to capital to fund the shortfalls. Lack of capital is a particular additional handicap in franchises in which the franchisor supplies the products as this will tie-up capital in large inventories. Franchising is not a solution to its problems for a company which is in financial difficulty and it would be foolish to become involved with a franchisor whose business has such problems.

5. The franchisor may run its business badly.
The fact that a business operates as a franchisor does not insulate it from business error, even though the franchise may have a basically-sound structure. A prospective franchisee, must therefore be prepared with a different set of questions from those which would be asked if one were buying a conventional independent business.

It must also be understood that just because someone is a franchisor it does not mean that its business cannot fail, nor does it mean that you and the other franchisees are protected from failure. However, a well-tested and structured franchise offered by a properly capitalised franchisor does provide the franchisee with a better prospect of success than he would have if he were to go into business independently.

It should also be appreciated that taking a franchise is not a substitute for hard work. To succeed as a franchisee, as in any worthwhile business venture, it will take a lot of hard work, complete commitment to the business, and the patience to allow time for the business to become established. There is no such thing in franchising as overnight riches or success.

In assessing a franchise opportunity, one must consider the following factors which are all of prime importance.

- Examine the franchisor's financial position in great detail. An accountant will be able to provide help. The prospective franchisee should satisfy himself that the franchisor has spent money on proving that his concept works in practice, and that he is adequately capitalised and financed to sustain the business in the future.

- Check how thoroughly he has market tested the business.

- Assess how well the system works in practice. Are the existing franchisees (if any) pleased with their businesses and the performance of the franchisor? Speak to existing franchisees - you choose those to whom you wish to speak. Don't let the franchisor choose them for you.

- Does the business have staying power, or is it based on something which is temporarily fashionable?

- Do not buy a franchise from anyone other than the franchisor. Do not deal with franchise brokers, save for advisers who provide an introduction or advice on what is available in the market. Remember that they may be retained by franchisors in whose propositions they will try to interest you. They also tend only to be interested in making sales and are not around later when problems may arise.

- Ask your solicitor to check the franchise agreement, preferably one who has experience in the field. The British Franchise Association has a category of affiliate membership which contains a list of solicitors with franchising experience. A franchisor needs to have controls in the agreement to ensure the uniformity of the system and the quality of its products or service. The agreement should be fair to you and the franchisor, and it should cover the services which you have been told you will get from it. However, by nature the contract will be one-sided in many respects.

- Make sure that you appreciate that there is always the risk that you might not be successful in the business, despite the success of others. You may not perhaps be suited to the stresses and strains of being your own boss. Despite your good intentions you may not operate the system properly or show the commitment which is needed. Your family may find that the strain is difficult to live with, and put you under more pressure. Be sure that you and they can cope.

CHAPTER FOUR
Assessing your suitability to become a franchisee

EVERYONE who decides that he would like to have his own business should subject himself to a detailed self-examination of his attitudes, capabilities and long-term goals. Some factors in any such examination apply whether or not the business is a franchise, and some are specific to franchising. There are factors which are fundamental to the assessment. Every potential franchisee must:

- engage in this self-examination exercise,
- be completely frank and self critical, and
- not be deluded into pursuing his original desires regardless of what he learns of the proposed franchise opportunity; he must not lose his ability objectively to judge the correct answers to the questions which he must ask himself.

Consideration should also be given to a factor to which no attention appears to be paid when franchisee failure is reported in the media. Franchisees can be the cause of their own downfall. It should be borne in mind that at least 50 per cent of franchisees who experience failure are responsible for their plight. The provision by the franchisor of his know-how, system, and business format does not guarantee success. The franchisor provides what is basically a DIY business kit, but the success of its operation depends greatly upon the franchisee's skill and ability in maximising the opportunity which it presents.

This factor sometimes makes it difficult to ascertain the reason for failure, although there is now enough experience available to identify the characteristics which give rise to self-induced failure by the franchisee.

Any potential franchisee who engages in self-examination should be aware of these characteristics in case he recognises that he himself possesses one or more of them. What are these characteristics? They include the following. (The examples quoted have actually occurred.)

1. The franchisee who has previously been in business for himself, and possibly in the same type of business as the franchise system.

Such a person may have entrenched ideas of his own and thus be less receptive to the ideas of the franchisor and the disciplines of the system. It is not just a question of learning new ways; it is necessary to abandon former knowledge and maybe habits of a working lifetime - that is not easy. It is for these reasons that many franchisors will not accept as franchisees those who have previous experience in that type of business. Life being what it is there are exceptions, and there are some businesses where previous market knowledge and experience are essential. However, in such a case the acceptance of, and submission to, the disciplines of the franchise system are fundamental.

2. Franchisee complacency.

No franchisee can afford to be complacent. There have been cases in which franchisees have failed to make the necessary effort because, as they put it, "*I am now a boss and bosses don't work.*" The "*boss*" syndrome can be quite dangerous. Franchisees who have this problem behave in the way that they think bosses should behave, which they usually believe means spending without working and earning. No one can succeed on that basis. If the franchisee's expectations of business life as his own boss are along these lines he should avoid self-employment because if put into practice he will be doomed to failure.

3. The franchisee who loses his nerve.

This takes two forms:-

(a) The franchisee who simply loses his nerve when, after opening, the responsibilities and magnitude of the task of being a self-employed businessman dawn upon him.

(b) The franchisee who cannot live with the losses which many businesses make in the early days before they become established. This loss of nerve occurs even in cases where the franchisees have been warned that it will happen and have been advised to arrange their finances on such a basis that they have the working capital to sustain them during the unprofitable start-up period. A strong nerve is necessary to be able to cope with trading losses while building a business.

4. The franchisee who does not follow the system.

This is a phenomenon which is more likely to occur after the franchisee has been in business for a period of time and has become successful. He begins to believe that he and not the franchisor is the reason for his prosperity. In part, he will, of course, be contributing to his own success. Some franchisees are better than others and some are more prosperous than others because of their diligence and hard work. The danger arises where this leads to an arrogant belief by the franchisee that he knows best and where this in turn leads to a rejection of the franchisor's system and a desire to impose his will and effect changes without authority.

5. Interference from other family members, or well intentioned but busybody friends.

It is important that the franchisee should have the support of his family (particularly the spouse or partner), but support is one thing and interference is another. It can be appreciated that a spouse or partner will have the welfare of his (or her) partner at heart, but the spouse or partner should not usurp the franchisor's function, or take on the franchisor on behalf of his (or her) spouse or partner. That is a recipe for disaster. Many franchisors will wish to interview both husband and wife or partner, even when only one is applying for a franchise in order to make an assessment of the degree of support which is likely to be forthcoming, as well as the degree of interference. Busybody friends should be avoided like the plague. They should be politely kept apart from the business, especially those who profess to have an expertise which they consider to be of vital benefit to the franchisee. Above all don't listen to the "know all" you may meet in the pub. A person who is easily led and finds it difficult to reach decisions independently will find self-employment a dangerous undertaking.

6. The franchisee who expects too much to be done.
Some franchisees develop a feeling that the franchisor should be doing more for them on a day-to-day basis than is allowed for in the franchise system. The franchisee who previously had a job with a salary will have to accept that he is now dependent upon his own performance for his take-home pay. He may mistakenly believe if the going gets tough expect the franchisor financially to bail him out. A franchisor should provide fall back assistance to a franchisee with problems. He cannot be expected to offer a day-to-day presence, or the local involvement and initiative necessary to develop the business. These are the franchisee's responsibility and no prospective franchisee should enter into a franchise relationship if he believes that the franchisor should be involved on a day-to-day operational basis in the business. The exceptions are the franchise systems which specifically provide such involvement. (This could occur, for example, where the franchisor operates a central booking or ordering facility, or accounting system).

7. The franchisee who does not have the right aptitude.
This type of franchisee falls into two categories. In the first category are those who are so blinded by the attractiveness of the franchise opportunity that they do not recognise their own inabilities and deficiencies or, indeed, those of the franchisor. A franchisor can never know as much about the franchisee as the franchisee knows about himself. The franchisee must be honest with himself and the franchisor. If, for example, the franchise system needs the franchisee to be an active salesman, as many do, and he knows that this is something he would find difficult he should hesitate to become involved. On the other hand, a franchisee who likes meeting people and who finds that the

franchise of his liking will involve him in stifling administrative duties should think again. In the second category are also those who have perhaps been in employment at a senior management level and are not accustomed to rolling up their sleeves and working hard at the basics and at the sharp end of a business. The subsequent sale of a franchised business which has been taken over by a franchisee with the right aptitude and attitude often proves how wrong was the predecessor's attitude.

These then are the characteristics which signal problems for the prospective franchisee. Those who are counselling the franchisee, including the franchisor, should assist him in questioning whether he will fall within one or more of these categories. The characteristics should be kept in mind as a general background against which to proceed with the evaluation process.

Let us now consider a widely-voiced statement, "*Franchising is safer than independently setting up in business on your own account.*" This, broadly speaking, is correct. In the UK, this claim is borne out by the experience of members of the British Franchise Association as a whole, and of reputable franchise companies and bankers involved in franchisee finance. The annual NatWest/bfa survey sponsored by NatWest also supports this claim.

It is popularly believed that while 90 per cent of all new businesses fail within a five-year period, the comparable percentage in the case of franchises is not more than 10 per cent. This popular assertion is a step in the right direction, but it is an overstatement of the position. The anecdotal evidence from those most exposed to the market place indicates that the prospect of failure for a newly established franchised business is around one-sixth of the prospect of failure for a newly established non-franchised business.

However, there are dangers in making assertions about the high level of success in franchising generally. The potential franchisee may:-

(a) drop his guard when evaluating a franchise because he has heard such claims and come to trust the system as a whole, regardless of what may be the position in the particular franchise which he is considering;

(b) be lulled into the false belief that all he needs to do to make a lot of easy money is to sign a franchise agreement;

(c) ignore the fact that it is still necessary to select the right franchisor who has properly prepared the franchise for its marketplace and one who is right for the franchisee.

The lessons to be drawn are that each franchise must be considered on its own merits in the light, preferably (at the very least) of the guidance offered in this booklet and in the certain knowledge that franchising is not the easy way to quick riches. In life, nothing comes easily and this is certainly true in franchising. Most successful franchisees have worked very, very hard to achieve their success.

Franchising should reduce the risks inherent in opening a new business. This is because one of the main attractions is that the franchisor is selling the benefit of the experience he has gained in running his own business (or his pilot operation) and has detected and solved the problems with which any new business is always faced. Franchising should, therefore, provide the franchisee with a business system, which has a proven record of success upon which he can build. No franchise should ever be offered, or be considered as a work-free way of making money. If it is offered in this way, you should be suspicious, and if you regard it in this way, you should stop deluding yourself or being greedy and come to your senses.

It is surprising that there are a significant number of prospective franchisees who take proper advice before entering into a franchise contract, but who fail to heed that advice because it was not what they wanted to hear. In other words, they have already made up their minds when they take advice and despite what they are told it makes no

difference. This particularly applies with new franchise systems where the tendency is to believe that however badly structured and inadequately tested it is, getting in early is desirable because those in first make the most money.

This attitude is really only a manifestation of greed which prevents rational thought. While those 'in early' in a well structured and properly-piloted franchise may do extremely well, the risks are higher, as will be seen below, and the prospective franchisee must be prepared to take a deep breath, reconsider his position and say 'no' however much he is enamoured of the proposition unless objective investigation, coupled with sound independent advice confirm the necessary quality of the franchisor and his proof, by spending his own money, that he indeed has a well-tried, tested and successful business format.

The factors discussed are all important in the process through which all prospective self-employed businessmen should go before taking the plunge. Indeed, the prospective franchisee must not lose sight of the fact that in deciding whether or not to go into a franchise he is also deciding to go into business on his own account, albeit in a particular type of business which has been structured in a certain type of way.

The following questions should be asked and answered honestly.

- Do I understand franchising and what is involved?
- Am I qualified physically and temperamentally for self-employment?
- Will my age/health permit me to run the business long enough to recover my initial investment and to make the effort worthwhile? Conversely, am I too young to have the maturity to run my own business, and employ and direct people?
- Do I possess sufficient financial resources to enable me to start a business, and survive while it is struggling to become established?

Assessing your suitability to become a franchisee

- Do I have the nerve and force of will to survive expected losses while building up my business, or to cope with any unexpected set-backs?
- What are my natural aptitudes and skills? Does this franchise opportunity provide me with the right platform for me to exploit and maximise my strengths?
- Do I have the skills and ability to be a salesman?
- Am I at my best with mental or physical tasks?
- Do I mix well with people?
- Will I be able to handle staff?
- Do I have the ability and commitment to work hard?
- Am I prepared to work unsocial hours?
- How will my family be affected by my decision and the calls which the business will make upon my time?
- Do my family wholeheartedly support my proposed venture?
- Will any of my family be able, available, and happy to help me?
- Am I prepared to put whatever assets I now possess at risk? Can I stand the stress which may follow from taking such a risk?
- Am I able to raise sufficient finance?
- What am I looking for, and can I achieve it:
    a) job satisfaction?
    b) capital gain?
    c) lots of money; Is this a wise goal?
    d) an investment (absentee owner)?
- Will the business be sufficiently challenging for me over a period of time?
- Can I accept the disciplines of a franchise system?
- Will I resent the franchisor's authority?
- Do I possess sufficient ability to capitalise on the opportunities presented to me?

- Would I enter the ranks of the self-employed other than through the franchise route?
- Finally, what do I want to achieve in life?

It is vital for the prospective franchisee to subject himself and his attitude to the closest possible scrutiny. He should be sure he knows himself and knows what he is looking for. He should ensure that in carrying out the self-assessment procedures which are recommended that his particular strengths and weaknesses are relevant to, and would be effective, if put to use in the particular proposition which he is considering and the demands it will make.

CHAPTER FIVE
Weighing up the advantages and disadvantages

IN this chapter we will examine two aspects. Firstly, we will look at the advantages and disadvantages of franchising from the perspective of the franchisee. Secondly, we will review the factors to be considered in assessing the type of business which is the subject of the franchise proposition.

Advantages

1. The franchisee's lack of basic or specialised knowledge is overcome by the training programme of the franchisor.

2. The franchisee has the incentive of owning his own business with the additional benefit of continuing assistance from the franchisor. The franchisee is an independent businessman operating within the framework of the franchise system. This provides the opportunity through hard work and effort to maximise the return from his business and the value of his investment.

In all franchise networks there are three basic levels of performance, despite the fact that all franchisees are provided with the same raw material.

There are the high flyers who do extremely well, having the right attitude and approach, as well as some entrepreneurial skill which enables them to make the most of their opportunities. Then there are the average performers, who operate the system and basically achieve the anticipated performance levels. Their attitude and approach is sound, but they lack the flair of the high flyers. They will earn a decent living in line with their expectations. Finally, there are those whose performance levels are low. These are people who joined the franchise with the best of intentions, but they now lack the will or the aptitude, or have changed their mind and want to get out of the franchise. They clearly made a mistake in the first place by going into self-employment, and they perhaps deluded themselves into believing that their franchisor would remove all the risk for them.

3. In most cases, the franchisee's business benefits from operating under a name and reputation (brand image) which is already well established in the mind and eye of the public. Of course, there will be new franchise schemes which are in the process of being established and in which the name will not yet be so well known. This is a factor to recognise and to make allowance for. Picking a sound, newer franchise in its early stages can be a good proposition, but the risks are higher.

4. The franchisee will usually need less capital than he would if he was setting up a business independently because the franchisor, through his pilot operations, will have learned how to make the most cost-effective use of resources and to eliminate the risk of purchasing unsuitable items.

5. The franchisor provides the franchisee with a range of services which are calculated to assist, so far as is practicably possible, the franchisee in enjoying the same as or a greater degree of success than the franchisor has achieved. These services will include:

- The application of developed criteria for site selection and identification of a trading location or, if the franchise is based upon a mobile operation, the area within which the franchisee will draw his customers.

- Guidance to the franchisee to assist in obtaining occupation rights to the trading location, complying with planning (zoning) laws, preparation of plans for layouts, shopfitting and refurbishment, and general assistance in calculating the correct level and mix of stock and in the opening launch of the business.

- The training of the franchisee and his staff in the operation of the business format and the provision of an operational manual with detailed instructions.

- The training of the franchisee and staff in any methods of manufacture and preparation which may be appropriate.
- The training of the franchisee in methods of accounting, business controls, marketing promotion and merchandising.
- The purchase of equipment.
- Guidance in obtaining finance for the establishment of the franchisee's business.
- Getting the newly franchised business ready for trading and opened.

6. The franchisee receives the benefit on a national scale (if appropriate) of the franchisor's advertising and promotional activities. It is usual for the franchisees to make a contribution to the funds which are expended for this purpose.

7. The franchisee receives the benefit of the bulk purchasing power and negotiating capacity which are available to the franchisor by reason of the existence and size of the franchised network.

8. The franchisee has at his disposal the specialised and highly-skilled knowledge and experience of the franchisor's head office organisation while remaining self-employed in his business.

9. The franchisee's business risk is greatly reduced. However, no franchisee should be under any illusion that he is not going to be exposed to business risk because he is under the umbrella of a franchisor. All business undertakings involve risk and a franchised business is no exception.

To be successful, the franchisee will still have to work hard, perhaps harder than he has ever done before. The franchisor will never be able to promise great rewards for little effort.

The blueprint for carrying on business successfully and profitably can rarely be a blueprint for carrying on a business successfully without working.

10. The franchisee should have the services of the field operational

support staff of the franchisor who should be there to assist with any problems which may arise from time-to-time in the course of business.

11. The franchisee has the benefit of the use of the franchisor's patents, trade marks, copyrights, trade secrets, and any secret processes or formulae.

12. The franchisee has the benefit of the franchisor's continuous research and development programmes, which are designed to improve the business and keep it up-to-date and competitive.

13. The franchisor obtains the maximum amount of market information and experience which is available to be shared by all the franchisees in his system. This gives the franchisee information which would not otherwise be available to him because of its cost or inaccessibility. Indeed, all franchisees contribute to this common fund of knowledge and experience which is available to the whole of the network.

14. There are sometimes territorial guarantees in appropriate cases which protect a franchisee from competition from the franchisor and other franchisees of the franchise within a defined area around the franchisee's business address and in the case of a mobile franchise, a defined area of operation. This will invariably involve issues under UK and EU competition laws, which make such guarantees difficult in some cases. This needs to be the subject of legal advice.

15. The recognition by the banks of the advantages of franchise financing have made lending sources and terms available to franchisees which are more attractive than those offered to non-franchised new businesses.

Disadvantages

1. Inevitably, the relationship between the franchisor and franchisee must involve the imposition of controls. These controls will regulate the quality of the service or products to be provided or sold by the franchisee to the consumer. It has been

Weighing up the advantages and disadvantages

mentioned previously that the franchisee will own his own business. However, the business which he owns is one which he is licensed to carry out in accordance with the terms of his contract. He must accept that in return for the advantages enjoyed by him, by virtue of his association with the franchisor and all the other franchisees, control of quality and standards is essential.

Each bad franchisee has an adverse effect, not only on his own business, but indirectly on the whole of the franchised chain and as such, all other franchisees. The franchisor, will, therefore, impose standards and demand that they are maintained so that the maximum benefit is derived by its franchisee (and indirectly the whole of the franchised chain) from the operation of the franchisee's business. This is what makes it necessary for a franchise agreement to have a one-sided look to it.

This is not to say that the franchisee will not be able to make any contribution, or to impose his own personality on his business. Most franchisors do encourage their franchisees to make contributions to the development of the business of the franchised chain which their individual talent and qualities permit.

2. The franchisee will have to pay the franchisor for the services provided and for the use of the system, i.e. the initial franchise fee and continuing franchise fees.

3. The prospective franchisee may find it difficult to assess the quality of the franchisor. This factor must be weighed very carefully by the potential franchisee for it can affect the franchisee in two ways. Firstly, the franchisor's offer of a business-format package may well not amount to what it appears to be on the surface. Secondly, the franchisor may be unable to maintain the continuing services which the franchisee is likely to need in order to sustain his business. These aspects will be discussed in detail in a later chapter.

4. The franchise contract will contain some restrictions against the sale or transfer of the franchised business. This is a clear inhibition of the franchisee's ability to deal with his own

business but, as with most of the restrictions, there is a proper reason for it. This provision is in the contract because the franchisor will have already been most meticulous in its choice of the franchisee as the original holder of the franchise for this particular outlet. Why then should it be any less meticulous in its approval of a replacement? Naturally, it will wish to be satisfied that any successor to the original franchisee is equally suitable for that purpose.

In practice, there is normally very little difficulty in the achievement of successful sales of franchised businesses. Some agreements provide for the payment of fees to the franchisor to cover the cost of dealing with applications and training the new, replacement franchisees. Also, if the franchisor introduces the purchaser, as can be the case, there will probably be a fee to be paid for the introduction.

5. The franchisee may find himself becoming too dependent upon the franchisor and fail to produce the personal drive which is necessary to build up a successful business and to take full advantage of the foundations for business development which the system provides. Some franchisees lose their perspective. They delude themselves into believing that the franchisor has a duty to be so concerned about their particular business as to ensure that it has a flow of customers and to provide a day-to-day involvement which is inconsistent with franchising as a concept.

6. The franchisor's policies may affect the franchisee's profitability. For example, the franchisor may wish to see its franchisee build up to a higher turnover (from which it gets its continuing franchise fee), while the franchisee may be more concerned with increasing his profitability, which does not always necessarily follow from increased turnover.

7. The franchisor may make mistakes in its policies. It may arrive at decisions relating to innovations in the business which turn out to be unsuccessful and detrimental to the franchisee. This is why franchisors are always urged to market test innovations thoroughly in their own company-owned outlets and to be able

to demonstrate to franchisees the cost effectiveness of introducing new ideas.

8. The good name of the franchised business and its brand image may become less reputable for reasons beyond his own control.

Type of business

The position of the franchise in the market in which it trades is a vital consideration. You should not only look at the particular franchised business in relation to its own activities, but also make an assessment of the prospects for the overall industry or trade of which it forms a part. The franchise will either be dealing in goods or products, or the provision of services. The accompanying table contains a comparison of the various considerations which should help in making an assessment.

Do not underestimate the importance of the questions in the table. Make sure that the proposition has been well enough

Goods or products	Services
1. Are the products new? Have they distinctive advantages over their competitors?	Is the service to be provided a new one? Has it a distinct advantage over competitors' services?
2. Has the franchised business been thoroughly proven in practice to be successful?	Same
3. Is this a product distributorship, or agency, which is not really a franchise but one which is promoted as a business format franchise and thus suspect?	Does this service have a novel or distinctive element about it which clearly distinguishes it from other similar and competitive businesses?
4. Does it have staying power?	Same

Weighing up the advantages and disadvantages

Goods or products	Services
5. Is it in a market area which is in a decline?	Same
6. Is it in a growth market?	Same
7. Is it exploiting a fad or current fashion which is thus transient and short-lived?	Same
8. How competitive is the market for the particular products?	How competitive is the market for the provision of these services?
9. How competitive is the price of the products?	How competitive is the price at which the services are to be offered?
10. Can this competitiveness be maintained?	Same
11. What is the source of supply of the products?	Not applicable
12. How certain is it that the source of goods and products will be available for the future?	Not applicable
13. Are alternative sources of goods and products of comparable quality and price available?	Not applicable
14. Is there a trade mark associated with the goods and products?	Is there a strong, distinctive trade mark (or trade name if a trade mark cannot be registered) associated with the provision of the services? If a celebrity name is used, remember that celebrities come and go, and so too can the related franchise.

Goods or products	Services
15. Are the products produced by a patented invention?	Not strictly applicable, although it is possible for a patented product to be featured in a service business so this could still be relevant. Is the service based on an exclusive process?
16. Does the franchisor have its lines of supply properly tied up?	Not applicable
17. Is there adequate back up in terms of guarantees and service facilities?	Not applicable
18. Could the manufacturer or supplier easily bypass the franchisor and you, and set up his own competitive franchise?	Not applicable
19. What is the reputation of the goods and products?	What is the reputation of the service, or process?
20. What is the reputation of the supplier?	Not applicable
21. If it is a successful franchise newly imported from another country will it hold a similar appeal in the UK market? Has it been market tested in the UK by careful and thorough pilot operations?	Same

tested and for a long enough period of time for one to be satisfied that the market really exists and has long-term prospects.

Please do remember, and there is no apology for the repetition, one must not enter into self-employment and franchising if one is not prepared to risk losing all! No prospective franchisee should delude himself into believing that any franchisor guarantees his success and that he will underwrite a franchisee failure. The risk the franchisee runs is his. That risk must be fully understood and appreciated.

CHAPTER SIX
Essential steps in assessing your franchisor

THE assessment of the franchisor is a very important part of the process of making up one's mind about whether or not to take up a franchise and if so which to choose.

Do not assume that just because someone calls himself a franchisor, it means that he really is one.

Many who perpetrate frauds will often try to lull the unsuspecting into believing that what they offer is a franchise when it is not. One should not allow one's self to be misled, particularly by these promoters of spurious schemes who suggest that disproportionately high rewards will follow.

It is quite common for a person with a business to be approached by someone who feels that he would like to become a franchisee of that business. This is very often the first time that the owner of the business has heard of franchising and in such a situation he is totally unprepared and quite incapable of offering a viable franchise. Frequently, the response by the owner of the business is to rush out and ask his solicitor for a franchise contract.

There is, of course, more to franchising than a contract. That, in a sense, comes last after the commercial viability of the business as a franchise has been properly structured and established. So do not make the mistake of trying to rush the owner of a business into selling a franchise. There have been cases where an approach from a prospective franchisee has acted as a catalyst for the creation of a new franchise. But from the planting of an idea to the establishment of a viable franchise can take a considerable amount of time. Indeed, very few properly structured and piloted franchise systems can be ready for marketing in less than two years from the time the idea is first conceived.

If you, as a prospective franchisee, believe that the business is attractive you must be patient and wait until the owner has had the opportunity to develop a proper franchise system in which it would be safe for you to invest. Otherwise, you may well be contributing to your own downfall.

Most of the franchise systems on the market are likely to be at different stages in the development and maturity of their franchise. The more franchisees there are, the easier will be the task of assessment because there will be many franchisees to whom you can talk about what the franchise and franchisor have done for them.

In situations where the franchisor is just getting off the ground, greater care is needed in making a choice, but this does not mean that one should not take up such a franchise. New franchisees can and do provide splendid opportunities for those who take the trouble to investigate them properly and choose wisely. The accompanying table illustrates the different stages in the development of a franchisor and the problems which can arise at each stage.

Stages of development

Number of franchisees	Comments
1 - 10	The franchisor at this stage is still feeling its way. This is when it will be discovering whether it has been sufficiently thorough in pilot testing its concept. Has its pilot testing been wide enough and in sufficient representative locations and conducted over a sufficiently long period? It is very vulnerable at this stage to its inexperience in selecting franchisees. It will also be feeling impatient because it

Number of franchisees	Comments
	has invested its resources in preparing to market its franchise and will want to get on with selling franchises in order to develop some cash flow.
11 - 40	The franchisor has now overcome its first hurdle, but may be facing the problem of having among the first 10 franchisees four or five who are unsatisfactory. The reasons for this are explained in chapter three. The unsatisfactory nature of these franchisees may not yet be apparent, but they could already be taking up a disproportionate amount of the franchisor's time. At this stage, if the franchise has not been properly structured, various stresses and strains will emerge.

The franchisor will at this point be developing its organisational infrastructure to cope with the increasing number of franchisees and the growth of the business. Care must be taken to ensure that the growth rate does not outstrip the resources and capacity of the franchisor. |
| 41 - 100 | By now the franchise is relatively mature. The franchisor should be well organised and enjoying a reasonable return from its activities. It will now be turning its attention to laying the foundations for substantial expansion. |

Number of franchisees	Comments
	It will also be at the phase at which it will need to evaluate what is happening within the franchise. Does it need an updated approach? Does it retain its freshness and competitiveness? Certainly, it will be a very different franchisor from the one we saw at stage 1 - 10. Now it should be possible to see how capable the franchisor is at adapting to progress and change and how well it has serviced franchisees.
Over 100	The franchisor will now have reached maturity and all the relevant information with which to assess the franchise should be readily available. The existing franchisees will provide a valuable source of information about the quality of the franchisor as well as the franchise system and the relationship which exists between them. The ability of the franchisor successfully to adapt to change and respond to developments and opportunities in the market place should also be apparent.

Fundamental questions

What qualifies the franchisor to be a franchisor? What is there to suggest that it is able to discharge its promises and obligations?

To answer these important questions, the franchisor should be asked to provide the following information:

Essential steps in assessing your franchisor

1. What is your business background and experience and that of your directors and principal shareholders (or partners)?
2. A detailed history of the development of the business to date.
3. What steps have you taken to prepare your business for franchising? (This and questions four to eight are particularly appropriate for a franchise which is in the early stages of development and will become less relevant as the size of the franchisor's network grows.)
4. What knowledge or experience do you have of franchising and how did you acquire it?
5. How many pilot franchise operations did you establish before you began to offer franchises for sale?
6. How much of your own cash did you invest in establishing that your business was franchisable?
7. How can I be sure that you have adequately investigated the market place and that you have acquired sufficient knowledge so that I can be satisfied that I am investing in a thoroughly tested business which has had the experience of confronting and solving the daily problems which arise? Please explain why you consider that the number of pilot operations which you conducted was sufficient in numbers and range of locations or area of operation to prove that the concept works and that you are justified in commencing franchising operations.
8. Why did you decide to franchise, rather than develop your business by the expansion of your own operations?
9. What is the growth rate you are planning over the next five years?
10. What is your corporate structure? How well can it cope with the growth of your franchise network and what plans do you have for the expansion of your support staff and the development of your infrastructure?

11. Who are the senior executives who will be influencing and planning the growth and development of the franchise network and dealing with the franchisees?

12. Can you confirm that none of these senior executives has ever been:-
    a) involved as principal shareholder or executive in a company which has gone into receivership or liquidation, or had an administrative receiver appointed or an administration order made against it?
    b) bankrupt or made an arrangement with his creditors?
    c) involved in a franchise company which has experienced business failure?
    d) unsuccessfully involved in business as a franchisee?
    e) convicted of a criminal offence (other than a motoring offence not involving imprisonment)?

13. Details of the following:-
    a) How many franchisees do you presently have? May I have their names and addresses?
    b) How many franchisees did you have 12 months ago?
    c) How many franchisees, within the last two years, have:-
        i) had their contracts terminated by you?
        ii) terminated their contract with you?
        iii) mutually agreed with you to terminate their contract?

14. How selective are you in choosing franchisees? Please explain your approach.

15. A copy of your latest audited accounts.

16. Can you confirm that there has not been any deterioration in your financial position since such accounts were prepared? If confirmation cannot be given, please explain why not.

17. Confirmation that you have made arrangements adequately to finance your activities during at least the ensuing year.
18. Are you a member of the bfa? If so, which category of membership?
19. Have you applied for membership of the bfa or to join its provisional or development listing and been refused?
20. Who are your bankers? May I take up a reference from the bank for at least the level of my proposed investment?
21. Do you have any franchisee finance arrangements with any of the banks? If so, with which and may I have details?
22. Please provide at least two financial and business references, other than your bankers.

The views of existing franchisees and the experience they have had with their franchisor are always very important. However, and particularly (but not exclusively) in the case of early franchisees, beware of any franchisees who may have caused, or largely contributed to, the problems of which they complain. This problem was dealt with in chapter three.

You should take advice from your solicitor and accountant and they will help you place the replies you receive in perspective. But whatever the replies and advice you receive, you must satisfy yourself that the franchisor you decide to join is one who will provide you with a long-term business relationship and one in whose judgement you feel that you can rely.

CHAPTER SEVEN
Assessing your franchisor's business proposition

THE business of the franchisor has to be investigated. This investigation should be concerned with securing answers to the following issues.

- How is the business structured?
- What will the franchisor do to assist the franchisee into business?
- What are the operational factors which are relevant and have to be considered?
- What are the detailed procedures for getting into the franchise?
- What are the on-going services and how will they be provided?

At this point in the investigation the franchisee should be trying to ascertain the "nuts and bolts" of the franchisor's operational system and his methods of working.

In most cases, the franchisor will provide the franchisee with the services mentioned in chapter five in order to assist the franchisee in obtaining his premises and preparing them for the opening.

However, there can be cases in which the franchisor offers what is called a "turnkey" operation. This means that the franchisor obtains the site and fully refurbishes, shopfits and stocks the store before handing the franchisee the "key" against payment of the cost. In a turnkey operation, the franchisee, who will receive his training whilst his shop is being prepared, does not get involved in any way in the construction and fitting out work, although the franchisor will keep in close contact with

Assessing your franchisor's business proposition

him during construction and will keep him in the picture and consult with him about what is being done. The franchisee will, of course, be responsible for the cost of the fitting out, equipping and stocking of the business.

The following questions should be asked:-

1. What is the total cost of establishing a business under your franchise?
2. What does this cost include?
3. What capital or other costs will be incurred by me in addition to the cost of establishing the business?
4. Do I have to pay a deposit? If so, on what terms? Are there any circumstances in which if I do not proceed, I will lose my deposit, or any part of it? If so, please explain.
5. What initial franchise fee do I have to pay? What is it for?
6. How much working capital do I need? What is the basis for your calculation of this requirement?
7. How long will it take to set up the business from the time we sign the contract to when we actually open?
8. What initial services do you offer?
9. What training facilities are there and where do you provide them? How long will the training last and what will it include?
10. Who pays for the training? Who pays the expenses I incur in attending for training, including fares and hotel accommodation?
11. Do you provide training facilities for my staff. If so, on what terms? If not, who trains them, and if I have to do so how am I provided with the means to do so?
12. What level of gross profit margin should I expect to achieve? Please itemise the expenses which I shall

expect to incur? What level of turnover do I need to achieve break even and how long should it take to reach that level?

13. May I see actual accounts which confirm, or fail to confirm, your projections? Can they be relied upon? Or are they merely illustrations?

14. What financing arrangements are available and what terms for repayment will there be? What rate of interest will be required and will the bank or finance company want security?

(Note - The questions which relate to financial performance will probably be answered in a qualified way. Very few franchisors will be prepared to make representations or give warranties of what financial performance will be achieved. A franchisor should be prepared to disclose actual figures which have been achieved, in his operations or by franchisees, although he should not identify any franchisee who achieved the figures without that franchisee's consent. No franchisee should rely upon any financial projections as being a guarantee that they will be achieved. There can be many reasons why they are not achieved including the franchisee's own deficiencies. No franchisor can prepare projections for franchisees because no one can set targets which are dependent on the performance of a third party. The would-be franchisee must prepare its own projections which are a reflection of what he thinks he is capable of achieving).

15. Is the business seasonal? In the case of a relatively new franchise involving a seasonal business, particular attention should be paid to whether the pilot testing was of a sufficiently long-term nature to be certain that seasonal factors have been taken into account. In the case of a longer-established franchise, the position should be more clear.

Assessing your franchisor's business proposition

16. What opening support staff do you provide?
17. Do you provide an opening launch of the business? If so, what does it consist of?
18. How do you make *your* money?
19. Do you charge on-going franchise fees? What are they and how are they calculated?
20. Do you make a mark-up on product sales to your franchisees?
21. If so, how much, and what protection do I have against unfair and unjustified increases?
22. Do you take any commission from suppliers of goods or materials to a franchisee? If so, please provide details.
23. Do you receive any other income or commissions from other source based upon business dealings with your franchisees? If so, please provide details.
24. Will I be obliged to maintain a minimum continuing franchise fee, or to purchase a minimum amount of goods? What happens if I fail to meet this commitment? How do you calculate these commitments?
25. What advertising and promotional support do you provide?
26. Do I have to contribute to advertising and promotional expenditure which you incur? If so, how much? Do you provide an auditor's certificate or other proof that the sums you receive for advertising and promotional expenditure have been spent for that purpose?
27. What point-of-sale and promotional literature do you supply, and what do I have to pay for it?
28. What help will I receive in local advertising and promotions? What will it cost me?
29. Will I be able to obtain and motivate a sufficient

Assessing your franchisor's business proposition

number of competent staff? Will they require specialist skills and are such people readily available?

30. Which of the following continuing services will you provide after the business has commenced:-
    i) research and development,
    ii) market testing,
    iii) negotiation of bulk purchasing terms for the benefit of franchisees,
    iv) field support,
    v) performance monitoring,
    vi) general business advice,
    vii) advertising, marketing and

31. Are there any other continuing services provided? If so, please provide details.

32. Which of your field support staff will be my link with you after I have opened the business?

33. Can I meet him/her?

34. Can I meet some of your other field support staff?

35. Can I meet your head office team?

36. How long have they each been with you and do they have service contracts which will ensure continuity?

37. Please explain the procedure which you will adopt to get me ready to open for business?

38. Will you find me a site, or do I have to find it myself?

39. Will I own the equipment which I need to operate the business?

40. How soon will I have to spend money on replacing equipment or re-modelling my premises?

41. How many times in the past and at what expense to franchisees have you required re-equipping or remodelling to take place?

42. What will be the opening hours of my business?

43. What systems do you have for keeping franchisees in touch with you and each other?
44. Do you publish a newsletter?
45. Do you hold seminars?
46. Is there a franchisee association within your franchise system?
47. How will I cope with my accounting and record keeping?
48. What restrictions will there be on what products I can sell?
49. Do you provide instructional and operational manuals?
50. What will you do if by a clear mistake you misjudge my site, and it does not produce the anticipated figures, resulting in a loss?
51. What would happen if I ran into operational problems which I was unable to solve? What help would I get?
52. How can I be sure you will do what you promise?

Ethical trade body

The British Franchise Association (bfa), formed in 1977, has given a formal structure to franchising and raised standards of ethics and business practice. Full membership is open only to franchisors who have been operating successfully and have franchised outlets established successfully over a period of time.

The franchisor is investigated before being admitted to membership and he must accept and observe a strict code of ethical behaviour.

The bfa has a disciplinary procedure, which can be invoked against a member who acts contrary to its code of ethics, or otherwise engages in questionable practices. The bfa publishes a useful guide, *The Ethics of Franchising*, which explains the principles of ethical business behaviour in franchising.

The bfa has also established arbitration and mediation schemes to be available to assist in the resolution of disputes between a franchisor and franchisee. The bfa can be contacted at www.thebfa.org.

Final step

The prospective franchisee must weigh up and consider the advantages and disadvantages of franchising described in the earlier chapters, as well as the replies to the questions posed in those chapters, before making the decision on whether or not to enter into any specific franchised business venture.

A decision must also be made as to whether the advantages, such as the established business format, training and support provided by the franchisor, are worth having in return for surrendering some independence and submitting to the degree of outside control which is inherent in a franchise transaction.

The prospective franchisee must decide whether the particular franchisor is the right person with whom to do business. Also, he must decide whether he is personally and temperamentally suitable for this type of relationship.

The prospective franchisee may also consider the advice of his local bank manager, or a businessman whose judgement he respects. He should also certainly discuss the matter with his immediate family.

When all these relevant factors have been weighed up, the legal issues and the franchise contract considered, and proper professional advice has been taken, the prospective franchisee has to make his final decision. If he is not able to make his decision with confidence, after having heard all that his advisers have to say, he should consider whether he is, indeed, capable of running his own business, whether franchising is right for him and whether the particular business is the right one for him.

CHAPTER EIGHT
The Franchise Agreement

THE franchise contract is the document in which the whole transaction is drawn together. It must accurately reflect the promises made and it must be fair, while at the same time ensuring that there are sufficient controls to protect the integrity of the system. The contract is, of course, important, although it does seem to attract a disproportionate amount of emphasis. It must:-

- Deal correctly, in legal terms, with the various property rights owned by the franchisor.
- Contain the operational structure and controls.
- Provide the franchisee with security in his operations and in his ability to develop and sell an asset.

In the final analysis, it is an insurance policy for both parties if things go wrong. If the contract has to be read after signature by either party, it will usually be because there is a problem, and not because one of the parties has insomnia for which dull legalese may be a cure.

The personal relationship between the franchisor and the franchisee, together with their common desire to succeed in their respective roles as the business relationship develops, are far more important than the formal contract. In most franchise schemes, the franchisor will own:-

- A trade mark, or trade name, and the goodwill with which it is associated.
- A business format - a system recorded in an operational manual, or manuals which will contain elements, some of which are possibly secret and confidential.

- In some cases, formulae, secret recipes, specifications, design drawings and operational documents.
- Copyright in some of the above items which are in written form and capable of copyright protection.

The recruitment literature of the franchisor will certainly have indicated the nature and extent of the initial services he will provide; the range of continuing services upon which the franchisee will be able to call; and the cost of joining and belonging to his franchise system. We shall look at each of these factors in turn. Whether or not you are considering taking up a franchise with a bfa member you should obtain the bfa guide *The Ethics of Franchising* since it describes provisions in contracts which the bfa considers to be in conflict with its code of ethics. A franchisor, who is not a bfa member and whose contract does not meet the bfa's ethical requirements, may not be the right choice.

The initial cost should include all the items necessary to open for business. The franchisor will very likely charge a franchise fee to cover the cost to him of providing the initial range of services to the franchisee, as well as a charge for entry into the system. There can be no hard and fast rule as each system differs. Ignoring the lower end of the cost range, the average amount of the initial franchise fee can in practice range from five to twenty per cent of the total setting-up costs.

Continuing fees enable the franchisor to finance the provision of his on-going services and back-up. The average continuing fee charged by bfa members, which includes funds specifically allocated to advertising and promotional expenditure, is in the region of 10 per cent of turnover. It is vital that the franchisor should not have undisclosed sources of income at his franchisees' expense, nor should he be able arbitrarily to increase the cost of the products which he supplies to his franchisees. Franchise fees, however they are described, are essentially a payment by the franchisee to the franchisor in return for the services provided by the franchisor. They are the gross income which the franchisor receives for the provision of his franchise services and upon which his business depends to cover its operating costs and profit.

Most franchise systems provide for the advertising and promotion to be handled by the franchisor, who will receive from his franchisees a contribution for that purpose. The most common method of calculating this contribution is the same as for franchise fees, namely as a percentage of the gross sales by the franchisee. In some cases, a franchisor may include the advertising expense in the franchise fee and undertake to spend a percentage of the fee on advertising and promotion. There are also cases where local advertising, rather than national, is more important and a franchises may find that the franchisor does not seek a contribution, but imposes on the franchisee the obligation to spend a certain sum on approved local advertising.

Initial services

The nature of the initial services will vary, bearing in mind the type of business. Obviously, a van-based franchisee does not need site selection assistance, and conversely, a shop-based franchisee does not need to be taught how to contact his customers in the same way as the mobile operator.

The general principle is that the franchisor's initial services (including training) should be sufficiently comprehensive to set-up a previously inexperienced person in business so that he can trade effectively, in accordance with his chosen franchise system, as soon as he opens.

Continuing services

Having established the franchisee in business, the franchisor now has the responsibility to sustain a continuing range of services to support him. These include:-

- Performance monitoring to help maintain standards and profitability.
- Continuing update of methods and new innovations.
- Market research and development.
- Promotion and advertising.

- Benefit of bulk purchasing power.
- The provision at head office of a specialist range of management services.

Features of the contract

The normal features of a contract will be as follows.

a) **The establishment and identification of the franchisor's proprietary interests.**

This will clearly deal with such things as trade marks, trade names, copyright materials and the franchisor's business system and know-how.

b) **The nature and extent of the rights granted to the franchisee.**

This will deal with areas of operation and the formal granting of rights to use trade marks, copyright material, etc.

It is relevant at this point to mention **territorial rights**, since these create practical difficulties. There are two aspects to the problem which arises when exclusive territorial rights are a feature.

Firstly, there are the commercial considerations and these have caused many problems for franchisors over the years. It is very difficult to determine a territorial arrangement, which is fair to both parties, especially when the extent of the likely penetration of the market cannot be judged. Indeed, quite often even the total size of the potential market cannot be estimated.

In the past, many franchisors, who have chosen the exclusive territorial route, have found that there was no effective way of ensuring that the potential of the area was fully exploited. The effect of this is to harm the whole network. Quite apart from the fact that within the area a market and demand is being created by advertising and promotion which is not met by resources, the way is prepared for competition to move in and do better. Also, disgruntled customers, or potential customers, are not likely to look elsewhere within the same network for their requirements. The franchise thus gets a bad name.

The obvious response is to suggest that performance targets should be established. Since the assessment of fair performance targets is dependent upon the same factors as have to be considered in defining a territory, the problem remains basically the same. Additionally, if performance targets are set they should take into account the potential expansion of the business as well as inflationary factors. These are also difficult matters to deal with in a fair and equitable way.

Secondly, there are the legal considerations. The introduction of exclusive territorial rights is likely to make the agreement subject to the competition laws of the UK and the EU. These competition laws are likely to be applicable to other provisions in the contract. Examples include product ties (in certain circumstances) and restraints on competition. Under both systems (i.e. the UK and the EU) there are what are called Block Exemption Regulations. These give exemption from the impact of the competition laws if the terms of the regulation are complied with. It is anticipated that most franchisors will benefit from the exemptions. This area of EU and UK law is very complex and advice on its impact may be desirable.

c) The period of agreement.

The basic principle in which many believe is that the franchise relationship should be capable of subsisting on a long-term basis. There may be various reasons, such as the legal position in relation to the tied supply of products, for a relatively short initial period (say five years), but most franchise schemes allow for the franchisee to be able to exercise a right of renewal. If the agreement does not grant a right of renewal a prospective franchisee should proceed with caution. It may mean that the franchisor will not even be prepared to agree any renewals or will try to make renewal unreasonably expensive. There may be legal reasons why a contractual right to endless rights to renew will not be possible. Beware of agreements which grant a relatively short initial period with rights of renewal for which large additional fees must be paid.

d) The nature and extent of the services provided by the franchisor, both initially and on a continuing basis.

This will deal with the initial services, which enable the franchisee to be initiated, trained and equipped to open for trading. On a continuing basis, the franchisor will be providing services which should be detailed in the agreement (see Continuing services above), and he may possibly introduce and develop new ideas.

e) The initial and continuing obligations of the franchisees.

These will range from accepting the financial burden of setting-up in compliance with the franchisor's requirements to undertaking to comply with operating, accounting and other administrative systems to ensure that essential information is available to both parties. These systems will be described in an operations manual which will be introduced to the franchisee during training and which he will continue to have available as a reference guide after he has opened for business. The manual will be constantly updated as the system develops.

f) The operational controls imposed upon the franchisee.

The controls are to ensure that operational standards are properly controlled - failure to maintain standards in one unit can harm the whole network. Franchisees will rightly be alarmed if any of their counterparts fail to maintain standards and the franchisor allows them to continue to do so. Often operational controls are very detailed with a cross reference to the operational manual. The contract will contain the obligations and the manual will explain how these obligations are to be discharged and will contain details of how the franchisor's system is to be operated. Beware of relocation clauses which may appear innocent enough but which could entitle a franchisor to require a franchisee to close down and move to other premises. In effect, this could result in a franchisee being required to open a new business in a new location or lose his franchise! (The *bfa Ethical Guide* has guidance on this issue).

g) Sale of the business.

One of the reasons for the success of franchising is the motivation it provides to the franchisee, which comes with self-employment and the incentive by selling the business of making a capital gain. For this reason, the franchised business should be capable of being sold. However, there will always be controls. If there are none, it should be a matter of suspicion. After all, if a franchisor is highly selective when considering applications by franchisees, there is every reason for him to be equally selective about those who want to join the network by buying a business from an established franchisee. It should be borne in mind that when a franchisee seeks a purchaser for his business it is the only time that the franchisor does not recruit his franchisee. The criteria by which prospective purchaser will be judged by the franchisor should be set out in the contract. The procedure to be followed should also be described in the contract. Some franchisors insert into the contract an option to buy the business if the franchisee wishes to sell. If such a provision is inserted in the contract, it should provide for the payment of at least the same price as is offered to the franchisee by a bona fide arm's length purchaser. Any artificial formula which might enable the franchisor to buy at less than market value should be resisted.

h) Death of the franchisee.

In order to give the franchisee peace of mind, provision should be made to demonstrate that the franchisor will provide assistance to enable the business to be preserved as an asset to be realised, or alternatively taken over, by the franchisee's dependants if they can qualify as a franchisee.

i) Arbitration.

Arbitration is in reality private litigation with a judge (arbitrator) chosen by the parties. It has advantages in that the proceedings are private; the arbitrator chosen can be selected because of his special knowledge of the business, which is the subject of arbitration; the timing of the proceedings can be fixed to suit the parties' convenience; the parties may establish the rules for the arbitration and save time and expense in so doing. There are also disadvantages. Not every dispute under a franchise contract will be resolved by the decision of an arbitrator (e.g. the franchisor will not want an arbitrator to judge whether his quality standards and system are being maintained; the franchisor's right to an injunction may be impaired if the arbitration agreement does not reserve those rights to him; the wrong choice of arbitrator may result in a compromise decision which will not satisfy either party). Bearing in mind the long-term relationship involved in a franchise, those areas where genuine misunderstandings can arise may be considered suitable for arbitration (e.g. fee calculations, rights of renewal).

The bfa has had an arbitration scheme for many years. Full details can be obtained from the association (www.thebfa.org).

j) Termination and its consequences.

Invariably, there will be express provision for the termination of the agreement in the event of a default by the franchisee. The franchisee should be given the opportunity to put right minor remediable breaches so as to avoid termination, providing that he does not persist in making such breaches. The consequences of termination will usually involve the franchisee in taking steps to ensure that he ceases to display any association with the franchisor. The franchisee will no longer enjoy the use of the trade mark/trade name, and other property rights, owned by the franchisor. In addition, the franchisee will be under an obligation for a period of time not to compete with the franchisor, or other franchisees, nor will he be allowed to make use of the franchisor's system or other methods.

In a brief chapter, it is not possible to cover every aspect in detail. However, the points highlighted above will have explained some of the basic features of the franchise contract and should enable the reader to approach it in a reasonably enlightened way. **This book is not a substitute for proper legal advice.**

CHAPTER NINE
Raising the finance to buy your franchise

AS a prospective franchisee, you will be concerned to know how much, and from whom, you might be able to borrow money to finance your cost of buying a franchise and establishing your business, and to cover your initial working capital requirements.

No responsible franchisor will accept as a franchisee someone who has to borrow his total financial requirements, even if a lending source is willing to provide the full sum. Very few franchisors finance their franchisees; there are sound reasons why they should not. Finance should be kept out of the franchisor/franchisee relationship.

There have in the past been times when franchisees have found that finance was not so readily available as it is today, but since 1981 all the major banks have progressively entered the marketplace and the situation has changed. They all now have franchise specialists on their corporate staff, and are committed to encouraging the development of franchising and lending to franchisees in appropriate cases.

The reason why the banks have concentrated their interest on franchising is because they have come to recognise and acknowledge that it is a safer way of establishing a new business. Furthermore, with the proven concept and the "umbrella" of the franchisor's organisation, the ability of the business to generate sufficient profit to enable the franchisee to repay his obligations and to live comfortably is more readily appreciated in the City. This enables the banks to consider lending a greater proportion of the franchisee's setting up costs than would normally be considered appropriate.

Each of the banks which has entered the field has adopted the same approach with one recent notable exception with the appointment of a central unit to disseminate knowledge of franchising and individual franchisors to the bank's branches. The alternative would be to educate the whole branch network about franchising and in evaluating a proposition. This would result in an inconsistency of approach, which would be damaging and confusing, and cause the corporate know-how to be spread so thinly as to be incapable of being put to good use.

The centralised structure enables a consistent attitude to be established by the bank towards each franchise system and propositions can rapidly be evaluated. As a result, the local manager in the field, faced with a prospective franchisee borrower, can be provided, not only with a brief about the franchising system in general, but also about the specific proposition which he is being asked to consider. Thus, the bank's decision about whether or not to be formally involved in any franchise is taken by specialists with the requisite knowledge and experience.

Despite these advantages there have been some attempts at decentralisation and it remains to be seen whether this approach will work.

In some cases the bank's decision on whether to lend to a particular individual is taken at local level by the branch manager, who will interview and evaluate the applicant, in the light of all the relevant information about the franchise scheme and the franchisor, which he has received from his head office franchise department. In addition to this central fund of information, the branch manager will contribute to the decision making process his own local knowledge of the marketplace and, if the applicant is already a client of his bank, the latter's suitability for a loan to start-up in business for himself. There has also developed a much higher level of awareness of franchising at branch level within the banks which is proving beneficial. In other cases the lending decision is taken by one of the franchise specialists who then passes the franchisee to the appropriate local branch.

The banks' franchise managers are a good source of

information. In the course of their activities, they interview most of the franchisors who are offering franchises. This provides them with a perspective which not many can match, as well as an invaluable market awareness of what is happening. They will always be helpful, but you cannot substitute their judgement for your own and nor would they want you to. Although banks may well be identified with a particular franchise by the franchisor promoting the availability of a finance arrangement, the banks do not, of course, warrant its suitability for any particular person. The banks do point out that a prospective franchisee should make a detailed evaluation of the franchise before making his decision. The banks are merely making a decision on whether to lend, and if so, how much, based on all relevant factors within their relevant lending criteria.

As a prospective franchisee, you should ascertain whether the franchisor with whom you are negotiating has a relationship established with a bank. If he has you will be put in touch with either a member of its franchise team or your local branch manager with whom you can discuss your financial requirements. If more than one bank is involved, compare the offers of finance; there are likely to be differences in the terms of the offers which will be made, and you must select those which best meet your particular needs.

A word of caution - do not assume that, because a bank or finance house offers finance, you do not need to investigate.

In making finance available, no bank, or finance house, gives any assurance, guarantee, or warranty, that the franchise proposition is sound. Remember also your investigation of the franchisor is more up-to-date than the bank's enquiries upon which they would have made their assessment.

When taking up a franchise and adopting a career as a self-employed businessman, one is entering a business world of **risk**. The prospective franchisee must, after making his own enquiries, assess the risk for himself, and decide whether he wishes to run that risk in return for the benefits he believes he may obtain. The process by which a franchise is evaluated is, of course, a valuable aid in establishing which type of business and which particular franchisor is right for the prospective franchisee.

CHAPTER TEN
Summing-up

TO sum up, you must pay close attention to the following factors:-

1. Weigh advantages and disadvantages.
2. Assess yourself.
3. Assess the business.
4. Assess the franchisor.
5. Assess the franchise package.
6. Speak to existing franchisees.
7. Don't become so "besotted" with the franchise opportunity that you lose all objectivity.
8. Consider and put into perspective the advice of others, who are qualified to give it.
9. Do not dismiss advice which is given because you do not like it.
10. Consider and consult your family.
11. Make up your own mind.

The following are danger signals, which either (as in the case of pyramid or other schemes) rule out the proposition, or indicate that you need to make a very deep and careful scrutiny of the particular franchise you are considering. So beware of:-

1. Heavy initial franchise fees.
2. Pyramid-type schemes.
3. Franchisors whose continuing fee income is too low to support the services with which they should provide their franchisees.

4. Contracts which do not match promises and are vague and lacking in detail.
5. The hard sell.
6. Franchises which are based on passing fads or fashions which may not have staying power.
7. A franchise consultant purporting to offer independent, objective advice, but who is, in reality, offering a franchise for sale on a commission basis or also advising franchisors. There is an obvious conflict of interest.
8. Get rich quick offers.
9. Franchisors who have not invested in pilot operations.
10. Fee arrangements where you have to pay a minimum fixed cash sum regardless of whether or not you do sufficient business.
11. Franchisors who have a significant number of franchisees who are not happy with the quality of their services.

Finally, good luck for the future with whatever decision you may make. If you do choose the franchise route, work hard in every aspect of your new business, and also in your relations with your family. Their moral, and practical support, will be a key factor in your success in your new business.

APPENDIX A
British Franchise Association Code of Ethics

THIS European Code of Ethics is the up-to-date version of the Code first elaborated in 1972 by the European Franchise Federation (EFF).

Each National Association or Federation member of the EFF has participated in its writing and will ensure its promotions, interpretation and adaptation in its own country.

This Code of Ethics is meant to be a practical ensemble of essential provisions of fair behaviour for Franchise practitioners in Europe.

1. DEFINITION OF FRANCHISING

Franchising is a system of marketing goods and/or services and/or technology, which is based upon a close and ongoing collaboration between legally and financially separate and independent undertakings, the Franchisor and its individual Franchisees, whereby the Franchisor grants its individual Franchisee the right, and imposes the obligation, to conduct a business in accordance with the Franchisor's concept.

The right entitles and compels the Individual Franchisee, in exchange for a direct or indirect financial consideration, to use the Franchisor's trade name, and/or trade mark and/or service mark, *know-how, business and technical methods, procedural system, and other industrial and/or intellectual property rights, supported by continuing provision of commercial and technical assistance, within the framework and for the term of a written franchise agreement, concluded between parties for this purpose.

2. GUIDING PRINCIPLES

2.1 The Franchisor is the initiator of a franchise network, composed of itself and its individual Franchisees, of which the Franchisor is the long-term guardian.

2.2 **The obligations of the Franchisor**
The Franchisor shall:

- have operated a business concept with success, for a reasonable time and in at least one pilot unit before starting its franchise network.

- be the owner, or have legal rights to the use, of its network's trade name, trade mark or other distinguishing identification.

- provide the Individual Franchisee with initial training and continuing commercial and/or technical assistance during the entire life of the agreement.

Appendix A

2.3 **The obligations of the Individual Franchisee**
The Individual Franchisee shall:

- devote its best endeavours to the growth of the franchise business and to the maintenance of the common identity and reputation of the franchise network.

- supply the Franchisor with verifiable operating data to facilitate the determination of performance and the financial statements necessary for effective management guidance, and allow the Franchisor, and/or its agents, to have access to the individual Franchisee's premises and records at the Franchisor's request and at reasonable times.

- not disclose to third parties the know-how provided by the Franchisor, neither during nor after termination of the agreement.

2.4 **The ongoing obligations of both parties:**
- Parties shall exercise fairness in their dealings with each other. The Franchisor shall give written notice to its Individual Franchisees of any contractual breach and, where appropriate, grant reasonable time to remedy default.

- Parties should resolve complaints, grievances and disputes with good faith and goodwill through fair and reasonable direct communication and negotiation.

3. RECRUITMENT, ADVERTISING AND DISCLOSURE

3.1 Advertising for the recruitment of Individual Franchisees shall be free of ambiguity and misleading statements.

3.2 Any recruitment, advertising and publicity material, containing direct or indirect references to future possible results, figures or earnings to be expected by Individual Franchisees, shall be objective and shall not be misleading.

3.3 In order to allow prospective Individual Franchisees to enter into any binding document with full knowledge, they shall be given a copy of the present Code of Ethics as well as full and accurate written disclosure of all information material to the franchise relationship, within a reasonable time prior to the execution of these binding documents.

3.4 If a Franchisor imposes a pre-contract on a candidate Individual Franchisee, the following principles should be respected:
  - prior to the signing of any pre-contract, the candidate Individual Franchisee should be given written information on its purpose and on any consideration he/she may be required to pay to the Franchisor to cover the latter's actual expenses, incurred during and with respect to the pre-contract phase; if the agreement is executed, the said consideration should be reimbursed by the Franchisor or set off against a possible entry fee to be paid by the Individual Franchisee;
  - the Pre-contract shall define its term and include a termination clause;

Appendix A

- the Franchisor can impose non-competition and/or secrecy clauses to protect its know-how and identity.

4. SELECTION OF INDIVIDUAL FRANCHISEES

A Franchisor should select and accept as Individual Franchisees only those who, upon reasonable investigation, appear to possess the basic skills, education, personal qualities and financial resources sufficient to carry on the franchised business.

5. THE FRANCHISE AGREEMENT

5.1 The Franchise agreement shall comply with the National law, European community law and this Code of Ethics and any national Extensions thereto.

5.2 The agreement shall reflect the interests of the members of the franchised network in protecting the Franchisor's industrial and intellectual property rights and in maintaining the common identity and reputation of the franchised network. All agreements and all contractual arrangements in connection with the franchise relationship shall be written in or translated by a sworn translator into the official language of the country the Individual Franchisee is established in, and signed agreements shall be given immediately to the Individual Franchisee.

5.3 The Franchise agreement shall set forth without ambiguity, the respective obligations and responsibilities of the parties and all other material terms of the relationship.

5.4 The essential minimum terms of the agreement shall be the following:

- the rights granted to the Franchisor;

- the rights granted to the Individual Franchisee;

- the goods and/or services to be provided to the Individual Franchisee;

- the obligations of the Franchisor;

- the obligations of the Individual Franchisee;

- the terms of payment by the Individual Franchisee;

- the duration of the agreement which should be long enough to allow Individual franchisees to amortise their initial investments specific to the franchise;

- the basis for any renewal of the agreement;

- the terms upon which the Individual Franchisee may sell or transfer the franchised business and the Franchisor's possible pre-emption rights in this respect;

- provisions relevant to the use by the Individual Franchisee of the Franchisor's distinctive signs, trade name, trademark, service mark, store sign, logo or other distinguishing identification;

- the Franchisor's right to adapt the franchise system to new or changed methods;

- provisions for termination of the agreement; provisions for surrendering promptly upon termination of the franchise agreement any tangible and intangible property belonging to the Franchisor or other owner thereof.

6. THE CODE OF ETHICS AND THE MASTER-FRANCHISE SYSTEM

This Code of Ethics shall apply to the relationship between the Franchisor and its Individual Franchisees and equally between the Master Franchisee and its Individual Franchisees. It shall not apply to the relationship between the Franchisor and its Master Franchisees.

*"know-how" means a body of non-patented practical information, resulting from experience and testing by the Franchisor, which is secret, substantial and identified.

"secret" means that the know-how, as a body or in the precise configuration and assembly of its components, is not generally known or easily accessible; it is not limited in the narrow sense that each individual component of the know-how should be totally unknown or unobtainable outside the Franchisor's business.

"substantial" means that the know-how includes information which is indispensable to the franchisee for the use, sale or resale of the contract goods or services in particular for the presentation of goods for sale, the processing of goods in connection with the provision of services, methods of dealing with customers, and administration and financial management; the know-how must be useful for the Franchisee by being capable, at the date of conclusion of the agreement, of improving the competitive position of the Franchisee, in particular by improving the Franchisee's performance or helping it to enter a new market.

"identified" means that the know-how must be described in a sufficiently comprehensive manner so as to make it possible to verify that it fulfils the criteria of secrecy and substantiality; the description of the know-how can either be set out in the franchise agreement or in a separate document or recorded in any other appropriate form.

Appendix A

■ bfa's EXTENSION AND INTERPRETATION

THIS extension and interpretation forms an integral part of the Code of Ethical Conduct adopted by the bfa and to which its members adhere.

1. Application

This Code of Ethical Conduct forms part of the membership agreement between the bfa and its member companies. It does not form any part of the contractual agreement between franchisor and franchisee unless expressly stated to do so by the franchisor. Neither should anything in this code be construed as limiting a franchisor's right to sell or assign its interest in a franchised business.

2. Disclosure

The objectivity of recruitment literature (clause 3.2) refers specifically to publicly available material. It is recognised that in discussing individual business projections with franchisees, franchisors are invariable involved in making assumptions which can only be tested by the passage of time.

3. Confidentiality

For the generality of this Code of Ethical Conduct, know-how is taken as being as defined in the European Block Exemption to Article 85 of the Treaty of Rome. However, for the purposes of Article 3.4 of the European Code of Ethics it is accepted that franchisors may impose non-competition and secrecy clauses to protect other information and systems where they may be reasonably regarded as material to the operation of the franchise.

4. Contract language

Franchisors should seek to ensure that they offer to franchisees contracts in a language in which the franchisee is competent.

5. Contract term

In suggesting in Article 5.4 of the European Code of Ethics that the minimum term for a franchise contract should be the period necessary to amortize those of a franchisee's initial investment which are specific to the franchise, it is recognised:

(a) that for a minority of the largest franchise opportunities amortizing initial investments may not be a primary objective for the franchisee. In such cases the objective should be to adopt a contract period which reasonably balances the interests of the parties to the contract.

(b) that this section could be subject to national laws concerning the restraint of trade and may need to be met through renewal clauses.

6. Contract renewal

The basis for contract renewal should take into account the length of the original term, the extent to which the contract empowers the franchisor to require investments from the franchisee for refurbishment or renovation, and the extent to which the franchisor may vary the terms of a contract on renewal. The overriding objective is to ensure that the franchisee has the opportunity to recover their franchise specific initial and subsequent investments and to exploit the franchised business for as long as the contract persists.

7. Adoption

This Code of Ethical Conduct comprising this Extension and Interpretation and the European Code of Ethics for Franchising was adopted by the bfa, replacing its previous Code of Ethics on 30th August 1990, subject to a transitional period for full compliance ending 31st December 1991. During the transitional period members of the Association are nonetheless required to comply at least with the Code of Ethics previously in force. In October 1991 the Association agreed with the European Franchise Federation some amendments to the Code agreed in August 1990 and at the same time extended the transitional period to full compliance to 31st December 1992.

> ● Franchisors in membership of the bfa are governed by a code of ethical conduct which comprises the European Code of Ethics for Franchising and the bfa's own "extension and interpretation" of the code. The European code was drawn up by the European Franchise Federation (EFF), the trade body of the national franchisors' associations of the individual European countries. This is a standard code, but each country has the opportunity to add its own extensions and interpretations, subject to the approval of the EFF. The code is endorsed by the Commission of the EC and came into force in Britain in 1992.
>
> Clause 3.3 of the code requires franchisors in membership of the bfa to supply a copy of it to prospective franchisees within a reasonable time prior to the signing of any binding document.

Notes

Notes

UNLOCKING LIFE'S ROADMAP: A PRACTICAL GUIDE TO SUCCESS

Sebastian Lee

SEBASTIANLEE

Unlocking Life's Roadmap: A Practical Guide to Success

CHAPTER 1: THE JOURNEY BEGINS

Life is an intricate tapestry of experiences, opportunities, and challenges. Each of us embarks on a unique journey, guided by our dreams and ambitions. In this chapter, we'll lay the foundation for your personal roadmap to success.

Success, in its various forms, is a destination many seek, but the paths to get there are as diverse as the individuals who pursue it. The first step on this journey is to define what success means to you. Is it a fulfilling career, strong relationships, financial abundance, or a combination of these and more?

Understanding Success

Success isn't solely about wealth or fame; it's about aligning your actions with your values and aspirations. Take some time to reflect on your definition of success. What does a successful life look like to you? What do you want to achieve? This introspection will serve as the compass that guides your choices along the way.

Setting Meaningful Goals

Now that you've envisioned your destination, let's set some goals to steer your journey. Goals give you purpose and direction. They can range from short-term objectives like acing an upcoming exam to long-term aspirations like starting your dream business.

Remember, the most effective goals are Specific, Measurable, Achievable, Relevant, and Time-bound (SMART). Write down your goals, no matter how big or small they may seem.

Embracing Challenges

Success isn't a linear path; it's filled with ups and downs. Embrace challenges as opportunities for growth. When things get tough, remind yourself why you started this journey in the first place. Resilience and determination will be your allies.

Continuous Learning

In this rapidly changing world, learning is a lifelong endeavor. Stay curious, read, seek mentors, and acquire new skills. Every experience is a chance to learn and improve.

Taking Action

Finally, remember that dreams remain dreams without action. The journey to success begins with the first step. Take that step today, no matter how small. Start building momentum, and you'll find your journey becomes more exhilarating with every stride.

CHAPTER 2: THE POWER OF MINDSET

In the previous chapter, we set the stage for your journey to success by defining your personal goals and understanding the importance of embracing challenges. Now, let's dive deeper into a fundamental element that can shape the trajectory of your path – your mindset.

Our mindset, the collection of beliefs and attitudes we hold about ourselves and the world, plays an incredible role in our pursuit of success. It's the lens through which we interpret experiences, make decisions, and ultimately, define our reality. In this chapter, we'll explore the various mindsets that can either propel you forward or hold you back.

1. The Growth Mindset

One of the most powerful mindsets you can adopt is the growth mindset. This perspective sees challenges as opportunities for learning and believes in the potential for development. People with a growth mindset understand that abilities and intelligence can be developed through dedication and hard work.

Take a moment to reflect on your own mindset. Do you tend to view challenges as obstacles that deter you, or as chances to improve and grow? Cultivating a growth mindset can make a significant difference in how you approach your journey to success.

2. The Fixed Mindset

Conversely, the fixed mindset is limiting. It assumes that our abilities are static, leading to a fear of failure and a reluctance to take risks. Those with a fixed mindset may avoid challenges to protect their self-esteem.

Identifying a fixed mindset in your thinking is the first step to transforming it. Embrace challenges as opportunities for growth rather than pitfalls that threaten your self-worth. Understand that failure is a natural part of any journey, and it doesn't define your capabilities.

3. The Abundance Mindset

Success often hinges on our perception of abundance. The abundance mindset believes that there are limitless opportunities, resources, and success to go around. When you operate from this perspective, you're more likely to collaborate, take calculated risks, and remain optimistic in the face of setbacks.

Conversely, the scarcity mindset assumes that there's a finite amount of success, leading to competition, jealousy, and a fear of missing out. Recognize when you're operating from a scarcity mindset and work to shift your focus toward abundance.

4. The Resilient Mindset

Resilience is a critical component of success. It's the ability to bounce back from adversity and keep moving forward. Developing resilience involves acknowledging your emotions, seeking support when needed, and maintaining a positive outlook.

5. The Empathetic Mindset

Success is often intertwined with our ability to relate to and connect with others. The empathetic mindset recognizes the value of understanding different perspectives, building strong relationships, and collaborating effectively. Empathy can open doors and create opportunities that might not be available otherwise.

As you embark on your journey, remember that your mindset is not set in stone. You have the power to shape and evolve it over time. Embrace the growth mindset, cultivate abundance and resilience, and foster empathy in your interactions with others. Your mindset will be the compass that guides you through the challenges and triumphs that lie ahead.

CHAPTER 3: THE ART OF GOAL SETTING

In the previous chapters, we laid the foundation for your journey to success by defining your goals and exploring the power of mindset. Now, let's delve into the art of goal setting—a crucial skill that will help you navigate your path with purpose and precision.

1. The Purpose of Goal Setting

Goals are the milestones that mark your progress along the road to success. They give you a sense of direction, motivation, and a clear focus on what you want to achieve. However, not all goals are created equal. To make them truly effective, they should be:

Specific: Your goals should be well-defined and clear. Instead of saying, "I want to be successful," specify what success means to you. Is it achieving a specific income level, writing a best-selling book, or becoming a renowned expert in your field?

Measurable: You should be able to track your progress and determine when you've achieved your goal. For instance, if your goal is to increase your income, you can measure it by setting a specific target, such as earning $100,000 per year.

Achievable: Your goals should be challenging but attainable. Setting goals that are too ambitious can lead to frustration and disappointment. Consider your current resources, skills, and timeframe when setting goals.

Relevant: Ensure that your goals align with your overall vision of success. They should contribute to your long-term objectives and be meaningful to you.

Time-bound: Set deadlines for your goals. This creates a sense of urgency and helps you stay committed. For example, if you want to write a book, set a timeline for completing each chapter.

2. Types of Goals

There are various types of goals you can set in different areas of your life:

Career Goals: These relate to your professional ambitions, such as achieving a promotion, starting a business, or changing careers.

Personal Development Goals: These focus on improving yourself, whether it's learning a new skill, developing better habits, or increasing your emotional intelligence.

Financial Goals: Financial success is often a significant aspect of overall success. Your financial goals could include saving for retirement, paying off debt, or investing in assets.

Relationship Goals: Success isn't only about personal achievements but also about nurturing meaningful relationships. Consider goals related to strengthening your bonds with family, friends, or your romantic partner.

Health and Wellness Goals: Your physical and mental well-being are essential for a successful life. Set goals for maintaining a healthy lifestyle, exercising regularly, and managing stress.

3. The Goal-Setting Process

To effectively set and achieve your goals, follow these steps:

a. Identify Your Goals: Take time to reflect on what you want to achieve in each area of your life. Write down your goals, ensuring they meet the SMART criteria.

b. Prioritize Your Goals: Not all goals can be pursued simultaneously. Prioritize them based on their importance and feasibility.

c. Break Goals into Smaller Steps: Large goals can be overwhelming. Divide them into smaller, manageable tasks. This makes progress more tangible and less daunting.

d. Create an Action Plan: Outline the specific actions you need to take to reach your goals. Assign deadlines to these actions to stay accountable.

e. Monitor and Adjust: Regularly review your progress. Celebrate your achievements, and don't be afraid to adjust your goals or strategies if needed.

4. Stay Committed

Goal setting is not a one-time task; it's an ongoing process. Stay committed to your goals, stay adaptable, and keep refining your approach as you learn and grow.

CHAPTER 4: THE ROADMAP TO RESILIENCE

In the journey to success, there's one companion you can't afford to leave behind: resilience. It's that remarkable quality that allows some individuals to bounce back from adversity, stay motivated, and ultimately reach their goals. In this chapter, we'll explore the vital role of resilience and how to develop it as a key asset on your path to success.

Understanding Resilience

Resilience is not a fixed trait; it's a skill that can be cultivated and honed over time. It's the ability to adapt and thrive in the face of challenges, setbacks, and adversity. Resilient individuals view difficulties as opportunities for growth and learning rather than insurmountable obstacles.

The Components of Resilience

Resilience consists of several interconnected components, each contributing to your ability to weather life's storms:

1. Self-awareness: Understanding your strengths, weaknesses, and emotional triggers is essential. Self-awareness allows you to recognize when you're facing adversity and how you typically respond to it.

2. Problem-solving: Resilience involves the capacity to assess

challenges and create effective strategies to overcome them. This may involve seeking advice, gathering information, or breaking problems into smaller, manageable parts.

3. Emotional regulation: Emotions are a natural part of the human experience, and resilience doesn't mean suppressing them. It's about managing your emotions constructively, so they don't overwhelm you. Techniques like mindfulness and deep breathing can be helpful.

4. Social support: Building a network of supportive friends, family, or mentors can provide crucial emotional and practical assistance during tough times. Having someone to talk to, seek advice from, or lean on can make a world of difference.

Developing Resilience

Now, let's explore how to cultivate and strengthen your resilience:

1. Embrace adversity: Instead of avoiding or fearing challenges, embrace them as opportunities for growth. Remember that even failures can provide valuable lessons.

2. Cultivate a growth mindset: As discussed in Chapter 2, a growth mindset can help you view challenges as opportunities for learning and development.

3. Build a support network: Surround yourself with positive influences who can offer encouragement, guidance, and a listening ear when needed.

4. Practice self-care: Taking care of your physical and mental well-being is fundamental to resilience. Ensure you get enough rest, eat healthily, and engage in activities that bring you joy and relaxation.

5. Develop problem-solving skills: Enhance your ability to tackle challenges by breaking them down into smaller, manageable steps. Seek out resources and information to help you find

effective solutions.

6. Learn from setbacks: Every setback has a silver lining if you're willing to look for it. Analyze what went wrong, what you can do differently next time, and how the experience can contribute to your growth.

7. Maintain perspective: Keep a long-term view of your journey. Recognize that setbacks are temporary and that success often involves overcoming obstacles.

8. Seek professional help: If you find yourself struggling with resilience in the face of significant challenges, don't hesitate to seek the support of a therapist or counselor.

Resilience in Action

CHAPTER 5: THE ART OF TIME MANAGEMENT

As you journey along the path to success, you'll quickly realize that time is your most valuable resource. How you manage and utilize your time can make all the difference in reaching your goals. In this chapter, we'll explore the art of time management—a skill that will help you stay focused, productive, and in control of your destiny.

Understanding Time Management

Time management is more than just setting schedules and deadlines; it's a strategic approach to allocating your time effectively. It involves making conscious choices about how you spend your hours to maximize productivity and achieve your goals.

1. Prioritization

The first step in effective time management is prioritization. Not all tasks are created equal. Some are urgent, some are important, and some are both. The Eisenhower Matrix, a useful tool, categorizes tasks into four quadrants:

Urgent and Important: These are top-priority tasks that demand immediate attention, like crises or deadlines.
Important but Not Urgent: These tasks contribute to long-term success but don't require immediate action, such as strategic

planning or skill development.

Urgent but Not Important: These tasks may feel urgent but don't contribute significantly to your goals. They often involve distractions and interruptions.

Not Urgent and Not Important: These tasks are time-wasters and should be minimized or eliminated.

By categorizing tasks in this way, you can focus on what truly matters and avoid getting caught up in less meaningful activities.

2. Planning and Organization

Once you've identified your priorities, it's time to plan and organize your time effectively:

Set Clear Goals: Having clear, specific goals guides your daily activities. Define what you want to achieve, both short-term and long-term.

Create a To-Do List: Make a list of tasks and prioritize them based on importance and deadlines. Break larger tasks into smaller, manageable steps.

Time Blocking: Allocate specific time blocks for tasks and activities. This minimizes multitasking and helps maintain focus.

3. Avoiding Time Wasters

Identify common time wasters and take steps to mitigate them:

Limit Distractions: Turn off notifications on your devices, close unnecessary tabs, and create a dedicated workspace free from interruptions.

Delegate: If possible, delegate tasks that others can handle, freeing up your time for more critical activities.

Saying No: Learn to decline commitments that don't align with your goals. Saying no is a powerful tool for time management.

4. Time Management Tools

There are numerous tools and techniques to assist with time management:

Time Management Apps: Utilize apps and software like calendar apps, task managers, and productivity tools to help streamline your schedule.

Time Tracking: Monitor how you spend your time to identify areas for improvement. There are apps and software designed for this purpose.

Pomodoro Technique: This method involves working in short, focused intervals (typically 25 minutes) followed by short breaks to enhance productivity.

5. Adaptability

Flexibility is essential in time management. Unexpected events and changes in priorities will occur. Be ready to adjust your schedule and priorities accordingly without becoming overwhelmed.

The Value of Time Management

Effective time management is not about squeezing more tasks into your day but about making deliberate choices to allocate your time where it matters most. It allows you to strike a balance between work, personal life, and self-care while progressing toward your goals.

Time management is a skill that will serve you throughout your journey to success, enabling you to make the most of every moment. In the upcoming chapters, we'll explore how to apply these principles to various aspects of your life, helping you stay on track and make steady progress toward your dreams.

CHAPTER 6: EFFECTIVE COMMUNICATION SKILLS

Communication is the lifeblood of human interaction. Whether in your personal relationships or professional endeavors, your ability to communicate effectively can be the difference between success and misunderstanding. In this chapter, we'll explore the art of effective communication and how it can serve as a powerful tool on your journey to success.

The Power of Communication

Effective communication is a skill that goes far beyond words. It encompasses verbal and non-verbal cues, active listening, and empathy. Here's why it's so vital:

1. Building Relationships

Success often depends on the strength of your relationships. The ability to communicate openly and authentically fosters trust and connection with others, whether it's with colleagues, mentors, or loved ones.

2. Conflict Resolution

Misunderstandings and conflicts are inevitable in life. Effective communication enables you to navigate these challenges, find common ground, and resolve disputes constructively.

3. Career Advancement

In the professional realm, strong communication skills are highly valued. They enhance your ability to convey ideas, lead teams, and influence decision-makers.

4. Personal Growth

Clear and thoughtful communication helps you express your needs, set boundaries, and articulate your goals. It empowers you to advocate for yourself and your aspirations.

5. Active Listening

One of the most crucial aspects of effective communication is active listening. This involves giving your full attention to the speaker, without judgment or interruption. It shows respect and allows for deeper understanding.

Keys to Effective Communication

To enhance your communication skills, consider these essential elements:

1. Clarity

Be clear and concise in your communication. Avoid jargon or overly complex language. Ensure your message is easily understood by your intended audience.

2. Empathy

Put yourself in the shoes of the person you're communicating with. Understand their perspective, feelings, and needs. This helps you tailor your message and respond with empathy.

3. Non-Verbal Communication

Pay attention to your body language, tone of voice, and facial expressions. These non-verbal cues often convey more than words alone.

4. Confidence

Confidence in your communication can make a significant difference. Maintain good posture, make eye contact, and speak with assurance.

5. Feedback

Be open to feedback from others. Constructive criticism can help you improve your communication skills. Encourage honest feedback from those you trust.

6. Practice Active Listening

When listening, focus on the speaker, avoid interrupting, and ask clarifying questions to ensure you understand their message.

7. Tailor Your Message

Consider your audience when communicating. Adapt your message to their needs and preferences. What works in one context may not work in another.

8. Practice Public Speaking

Public speaking is a valuable skill that can boost your confidence and effectiveness in various situations. Consider joining a public speaking group or seeking out opportunities to present in front of others.

Communication in Action

As you progress through this book, you'll find that effective communication is woven into the fabric of success. Whether you're networking, leading a team, or negotiating a deal, your ability to communicate clearly and empathetically will be your guiding star.

In the chapters to come, we'll explore how to apply these

communication skills in diverse scenarios, from leadership and teamwork to personal growth and conflict resolution. Effective communication is the bridge that connects you to your goals and the people who can help you reach them.

CHAPTER 7: THE ART OF NETWORKING AND BUILDING RELATIONSHIPS

Success in today's interconnected world often hinges on your ability to build and nurture relationships. Whether you're advancing in your career, starting a business, or seeking personal growth, networking and relationship-building are invaluable skills. In this chapter, we'll explore the art of networking and how it can be a catalyst for your journey to success.

The Power of Networking

Networking is more than just attending social events or collecting business cards; it's about creating meaningful connections with people who can support and enrich your life in various ways. Here's why networking matters:

1. Opportunities Abound

Networking exposes you to a world of opportunities. Whether it's job openings, collaborative projects, or new friendships, the connections you make can open doors that you might not have discovered on your own.

2. Learning and Growth

Interacting with diverse individuals allows you to learn from their experiences, perspectives, and knowledge. It's a continuous source of personal and professional growth.

3. Support and Resources

Your network can provide essential support during challenging times. They can offer advice, mentorship, and even emotional encouragement when you need it most.

4. Influence and Impact

Building a strong network can enhance your ability to influence decisions and make an impact in your field of interest. It's a powerful tool for those looking to effect change or create a difference.

Effective Networking Strategies

Effective networking is about quality over quantity. Here are strategies to help you build a strong and meaningful network:

1. Be Authentic

Genuine connections are built on authenticity. Be yourself when interacting with others. Authenticity fosters trust and lasting relationships.

2. Listen Actively

When networking, focus on listening rather than speaking. Show a genuine interest in others' stories and experiences. Ask open-ended questions that encourage them to share.

3. Offer Value

Networking isn't just about what you can gain; it's also about what you can give. Offer help, support, or insights to others in your network. It creates a reciprocal relationship.

4. Diversify Your Network

Don't limit your network to people in your field. Diversity in your connections can lead to fresh perspectives and unexpected opportunities. Seek out groups or events related to your interests and hobbies outside of work.

5. Maintain Relationships

Building relationships takes time and effort. Stay in touch with your network by sending occasional emails, meeting for coffee, or attending events. Nurture these connections to keep them strong.

6. Online Networking

In today's digital age, online networking is just as important as in-person interactions. Use platforms like LinkedIn to connect with professionals in your field, share your expertise, and join relevant groups.

7. Attend Networking Events

Attend conferences, workshops, and industry-related events. These gatherings provide a fertile ground for meeting like-minded individuals and potential mentors.

8. Follow Up

After making a new connection, follow up with a thank-you email or message. Express your gratitude for their time and express your interest in maintaining the relationship.

Networking in Action

As you progress through this book, you'll discover that networking and relationship-building skills are intertwined with every aspect of success. Whether you're seeking career advancement, entrepreneurial opportunities, or personal development, your network will be a valuable resource.

In the upcoming chapters, we'll explore how to apply these

networking skills in various contexts, from professional growth and leadership to collaboration and personal support. Remember, your network is a reflection of your journey, and each connection is a stepping stone on your path to success.

CHAPTER 8: THE ART OF LEADERSHIP AND INFLUENCE

Leadership is more than just a title; it's a set of skills and qualities that empower you to guide and inspire others toward a common goal. Whether you're leading a team, a project, or your own life, effective leadership can be a cornerstone of your journey to success. In this chapter, we'll explore the art of leadership and how it can elevate your path.

Understanding Leadership

Leadership isn't about exerting authority or control over others; it's about inspiring them to willingly follow your lead. Effective leaders possess a combination of traits and skills that make them influential and respected. Here's why leadership is essential on your path to success:

1. Inspiring Action

Leaders have the ability to inspire action and motivate others to achieve shared objectives. They provide a vision that people can rally around and work toward together.

2. Decision-Making

Leaders are often responsible for making critical decisions. Effective leaders are skilled at gathering information, weighing options, and making choices that align with their goals.

3. Problem Solving

Leaders encounter challenges and obstacles, but they approach them with a problem-solving mindset. They seek solutions, adapt to change, and find ways to overcome adversity.

4. Communication

As we explored in the previous chapters, effective communication is a vital aspect of leadership. Leaders must articulate their vision, provide guidance, and listen to the concerns and ideas of their team.

5. Building and Empowering Teams

Leaders are only as successful as the teams they lead. A crucial skill is building a cohesive, motivated team and empowering individuals to excel.

Qualities of Effective Leaders

Effective leaders embody a range of qualities that set them apart. Here are some key leadership traits:

1. Vision

Leaders have a clear and compelling vision for the future. They can see the bigger picture and inspire others to work toward it.

2. Integrity

Integrity is at the core of leadership. Leaders lead by example, demonstrating honesty, ethics, and a commitment to their values.

3. Empathy

Understanding and empathizing with the needs and concerns of others fosters trust and cooperation. Empathetic leaders build stronger connections with their team.

4. Adaptability

Leaders must be adaptable in the face of change and uncertainty. They remain open to new ideas and flexible in their approach.

5. Resilience

Leaders face setbacks and challenges, but their resilience allows them to bounce back and lead with determination.

6. Accountability

Effective leaders take responsibility for their decisions and actions. They hold themselves accountable and expect the same from their team.

Becoming a Leader

Leadership is a skill that can be developed and refined over time. Here's how to start your journey as a leader:

1. Identify Your Leadership Style

There is no one-size-fits-all approach to leadership. Discover your leadership style, whether it's authoritative, collaborative, servant leadership, or another style that resonates with you.

2. Learn from Role Models

Study the leaders you admire. What qualities and practices do they possess? Learn from their successes and challenges.

3. Seek Feedback

Ask for feedback from colleagues, mentors, and team members. Constructive feedback can help you identify areas for improvement.

4. Practice Decision-Making

Make decisions, even if they're small at first. Practice weighing options and considering the consequences.

5. Build Emotional Intelligence

Emotional intelligence is crucial for effective leadership. Develop your ability to understand and manage your emotions and those of others.

Leadership in Action

As you progress through this book, you'll find that leadership is a thread that runs through every aspect of your journey to success. Whether you're building a career, leading a team, or pursuing personal growth, your leadership skills will guide you.

CHAPTER 9: MASTERING THE ART OF TIME AND PROJECT MANAGEMENT

In your journey to success, you'll often find yourself juggling multiple tasks, deadlines, and responsibilities. That's where the art of time and project management comes into play. This chapter will delve deep into these essential skills, helping you become more efficient, organized, and in control of your pursuits.

The Essence of Time Management

Effective time management is the cornerstone of productivity and success. It's about making the most of your limited hours each day. Here's why it's crucial:

1. Enhanced Productivity

When you manage your time well, you're more focused and less prone to distractions, enabling you to accomplish more in less time.

2. Reduced Stress

Effective time management reduces the feeling of being overwhelmed. You gain a sense of control over your tasks and deadlines, leading to lower stress levels.

3. Goal Achievement

Time management aligns your daily actions with your long-term goals. It ensures you invest time in what truly matters and helps you stay on track.

4. Improved Work-Life Balance

Properly managing your time allows you to allocate moments for both work and personal life, fostering a better balance and overall well-being.

Key Principles of Time Management

To master time management, consider these essential principles:

1. Prioritization

Identify tasks and activities that are most important and urgent. The Eisenhower Matrix, as discussed in a previous chapter, is an excellent tool for this.

2. Set Goals

Establish clear, specific goals for what you want to achieve. These goals serve as a guide for your daily tasks and activities.

3. Create a To-Do List

Compile a list of tasks and prioritize them based on importance and deadlines. Break down larger tasks into smaller, manageable steps.

4. Time Blocking

Allocate specific time blocks for different activities and tasks. This helps you maintain focus and avoid multitasking.

5. Limit Distractions

Minimize distractions by turning off unnecessary notifications, creating a designated workspace, and using techniques like the Pomodoro method.

6. Learn to Say No

Avoid overcommitting yourself. It's okay to decline additional tasks or projects when your plate is full.

Project Management for Success

Project management goes hand in hand with time management, especially when you're dealing with larger, more complex tasks or goals. It involves planning, executing, and monitoring a project from start to finish. Here's why it's vital:

1. Improved Efficiency

Project management streamlines the execution of tasks by breaking them down into manageable steps. It ensures resources are allocated efficiently.

2. Clear Objectives

Projects have defined objectives, timelines, and deliverables. This clarity keeps everyone involved on the same page.

3. Risk Mitigation

Effective project management identifies potential risks and provides strategies to mitigate them. It helps prevent unexpected setbacks.

4. Enhanced Collaboration

Project management encourages teamwork and collaboration. Team members have assigned roles and responsibilities, fostering cooperation and accountability.

Principles of Project Management

Here are some key principles to keep in mind when managing projects:

1. Define Objectives

Clearly define the project's objectives, scope, and desired outcomes. This sets the foundation for all project activities.

2. Create a Project Plan

Develop a detailed project plan outlining tasks, timelines, and resources required. Ensure all team members understand their roles.

3. Monitor Progress

Regularly monitor and track progress to ensure the project stays on schedule and within scope. Make adjustments as needed.

4. Communicate Effectively

Open and transparent communication is crucial. Keep all stakeholders informed about the project's status, challenges, and milestones.

5. Manage Risks

Identify potential risks and develop contingency plans to address them. This proactive approach minimizes the impact of unexpected issues.

Time and Project Management in Action

As you continue your journey to success, time and project management skills will serve as your compass, guiding you through the complexities of your goals and responsibilities. Whether you're pursuing a career, launching a business, or seeking personal growth, these skills will keep you organized, efficient, and on track.

CHAPTER 10: THE SCIENCE OF DECISION-MAKING

Every day, we make countless decisions—some trivial, others life-altering. The quality of your decisions significantly impacts your journey to success. In this chapter, we'll dive into the science of decision-making, exploring how to make better choices and navigate the complex web of options that life presents.

The Importance of Decision-Making

Decision-making is the process of selecting the best course of action from multiple alternatives. Whether you're choosing a career path, making financial decisions, or selecting your next project, here's why effective decision-making is essential:

1. Shaping Your Destiny

Your decisions determine the direction of your life. The choices you make can lead you closer to your goals or steer you off course.

2. Resource Allocation

Decisions involve the allocation of valuable resources, such as time, money, and energy. Effective decisions ensure these resources are used optimally.

3. Problem Solving

In every challenge or obstacle you face, there's a decision to be made. Effective decision-making is essential for finding solutions and overcoming obstacles.

4. Risk Management

Decisions often involve some level of risk. Understanding how to assess and manage risks is a crucial aspect of making informed choices.

Understanding the Decision-Making Process

Effective decision-making is a skill that can be honed. It involves a series of steps:

1. Identify the Problem

Begin by clearly defining the issue or problem that requires a decision. Ensure you have a complete understanding of the situation.

2. Gather Information

Collect relevant data and information that will help you make an informed decision. This may involve research, consulting experts, or analyzing past experiences.

3. Generate Alternatives

Brainstorm a range of possible solutions or choices. Don't settle for the first option that comes to mind; explore different avenues.

4. Evaluate Options

Assess each alternative based on its pros and cons. Consider factors like feasibility, potential risks, and alignment with your goals.

5. Make a Decision

Choose the option that aligns best with your objectives and

values. Trust your judgment and be prepared to commit to your choice.

6. Implement Your Decision

Once you've made a decision, take action. Create a plan and put it into practice.

7. Review and Adapt

Regularly review the outcomes of your decisions. If necessary, be willing to adapt and make changes based on feedback and results.

Factors Influencing Decision-Making

Several psychological and cognitive factors can impact the quality of your decisions. These include:

1. Cognitive Biases

Human brains are prone to various biases that can lead to irrational decisions. Examples include confirmation bias (favoring information that confirms existing beliefs) and anchoring (relying heavily on the first piece of information encountered).

2. Emotions

Emotions can cloud judgment. It's important to recognize and manage emotions when making decisions, especially in high-stress situations.

3. Heuristics

Heuristics are mental shortcuts that help simplify decision-making. While they can be useful, they may also lead to errors. Understanding when to use heuristics and when to engage in more deliberate decision-making is crucial.

4. Decision Fatigue

The more decisions you make in a day, the more mentally taxing it can become. Decision fatigue can lead to poorer choices later in the day. Recognize this and prioritize your most critical decisions when your mental energy is highest.

Improving Your Decision-Making Skills

To make better decisions, consider the following strategies:

1. Seek Diverse Perspectives

Consult with others and gather different viewpoints to gain a broader understanding of the situation.

2. Practice Critical Thinking

Develop your critical thinking skills, which involve evaluating arguments and evidence objectively.

3. Use Decision-Making Tools

Various decision-making tools, such as decision matrices and SWOT analysis, can help structure your choices and weigh options.

4. Learn from Experience

Reflect on past decisions and their outcomes. Use these experiences to inform your future choices.

5. Manage Stress

Implement stress-management techniques to ensure emotions don't cloud your judgment during decision-making.

Decision-Making in Action

As you move forward on your journey to success, you'll encounter a myriad of decisions. Whether they're related to your career, relationships, or personal growth, your ability to make informed choices will be a guiding force.

CHAPTER 11: THE ART OF PROBLEM SOLVING

Life is a journey filled with challenges and obstacles. How you approach and overcome these challenges can greatly influence your path to success. In this chapter, we'll delve into the art of problem solving—a skill that equips you to tackle complex issues, make informed decisions, and navigate the twists and turns of your journey.

The Significance of Problem Solving

Problem solving is a fundamental skill that extends into every aspect of life, from personal development to professional growth. Here's why it's so crucial:

1. Effective Decision-Making

Problem solving and decision-making are intertwined. Problem-solving skills help you identify and analyze issues, laying the foundation for informed choices.

2. Creative Solutions

Problem solving encourages creative thinking. It pushes you to explore alternative solutions and think outside the box.

3. Adaptability

Life rarely follows a linear path. Problem-solving skills enable you to adapt to unexpected challenges and find solutions in dynamic environments.

4. Continuous Improvement

Effective problem solving fosters a mindset of continuous improvement. It encourages reflection and learning from your experiences.

The Problem-Solving Process

Problem solving is not a single step but a series of actions and strategies. Here's a structured approach to problem solving:

1. Define the Problem

Begin by clearly defining the problem or challenge you're facing. Ensure you have a thorough understanding of its scope and impact.

2. Gather Information

Collect relevant data, facts, and information related to the problem. This may involve research, analysis, or seeking input from others.

3. Generate Solutions

Brainstorm potential solutions or approaches to address the problem. Encourage creativity and consider a variety of options.

4. Evaluate Solutions

Assess each solution based on its feasibility, potential risks, and alignment with your goals. Consider both short-term and long-term consequences.

5. Choose the Best Solution

Select the solution that best addresses the problem and aligns with your objectives. Be prepared to commit to your choice.

6. Implement the Solution

Take action to put your chosen solution into practice. Create a plan and execute it effectively.

7. Monitor and Adapt

Regularly monitor the progress of your chosen solution. Be open to adjustments and improvements as needed.

Problem-Solving Strategies

Effective problem solving involves a combination of strategies and techniques. Here are some approaches to enhance your problem-solving skills:

1. Root Cause Analysis

Dig deep to identify the underlying causes of a problem rather than just addressing its symptoms. This helps prevent recurrence.

2. Critical Thinking

Critical thinking involves evaluating information objectively and making informed judgments. It's a valuable tool for problem solving.

3. SWOT Analysis

SWOT (Strengths, Weaknesses, Opportunities, Threats) analysis is a framework for assessing a situation from different angles and identifying potential courses of action.

4. Brainstorming

Brainstorming sessions with a diverse group of individuals can yield a range of creative solutions to a problem.

5. Decision Matrices

Decision matrices help you systematically evaluate and compare multiple options based on predefined criteria.

6. Feedback and Collaboration

Seek input and feedback from others who may have valuable insights or expertise related to the problem.

Problem Solving in Action

As you continue your journey toward success, you'll encounter a variety of challenges—some expected, others unforeseen. Your ability to approach these challenges with a structured problem-solving mindset will be your key to progress.

CHAPTER 12: THE ART OF INNOVATION AND CREATIVE PROBLEM SOLVING

Innovation is the driving force behind progress and success in our ever-evolving world. It's about thinking outside the box, pushing boundaries, and finding novel solutions to old and new challenges. In this chapter, we'll explore the art of innovation and creative problem solving, helping you unlock your potential to envision and implement groundbreaking ideas.

The Power of Innovation

Innovation is not limited to technological breakthroughs; it permeates all aspects of life, from business to personal development. Here's why it's so vital:

1. Competitive Advantage

Innovation can set you apart from the competition. It allows you to offer unique products, services, or solutions that meet the evolving needs of your audience.

2. Adaptation to Change

In a rapidly changing world, innovation equips you to adapt and thrive. It ensures you stay relevant and resilient in the face of disruptions.

3. Problem Solving

Creative problem solving is at the heart of innovation. It enables you to find fresh approaches to old problems and address new challenges effectively.

4. Growth and Exploration

Innovation encourages exploration and growth, both personally and professionally. It sparks curiosity and drives you to discover new horizons.

Understanding the Innovation Process

Innovation is not a mysterious process reserved for a select few; it's a systematic approach that anyone can learn and apply. Here are the key stages of the innovation process:

1. Identify a Challenge or Opportunity

Innovation often starts with recognizing a problem or a chance to improve something. It could be a business process, a product, or a personal goal.

2. Research and Gather Insights

Delve deep into the issue at hand. Conduct research, gather data, and seek insights from experts and relevant sources.

3. Ideation and Brainstorming

Brainstorming is a creative phase where you generate as many ideas as possible, without judgment. Encourage diversity in thought and explore unconventional possibilities.

4. Evaluate and Refine Ideas

Not all ideas are equally valuable. Evaluate each idea based on criteria like feasibility, impact, and alignment with your goals. Refine the most promising ones.

5. Prototype and Test

Create prototypes or models of your ideas to test their practicality and effectiveness. Gather feedback and make necessary adjustments.

6. Implementation

Once you've refined your idea and tested it successfully, it's time to implement it. Develop a plan and execute it strategically.

7. Continuous Improvement

Innovation is an ongoing process. Continuously gather feedback, monitor the results, and make improvements as needed.

Fostering Creativity

Creativity is the wellspring of innovation. Here are some strategies to boost your creative thinking:

1. Embrace Curiosity

Stay curious about the world around you. Ask questions, explore new topics, and seek out diverse experiences.

2. Collaborate

Collaboration with others can spark new ideas and perspectives. Engage in brainstorming sessions and exchange ideas with peers.

3. Create a Creative Environment

Design a workspace that inspires creativity. Include elements like artwork, natural light, and comfortable seating.

4. Mindfulness and Meditation

Mindfulness practices can enhance your ability to focus and think creatively. They help you quiet the noise and connect with your inner creativity.

5. Divergent Thinking

Practice divergent thinking by coming up with multiple solutions to a problem, even if they seem far-fetched. This exercise expands your creative horizons.

Innovation in Action

As you journey toward success, innovation and creative problem solving will be your allies in navigating the challenges and opportunities that arise. Whether you're a business leader, an artist, or an aspiring entrepreneur, innovation empowers you to chart new paths and find unique solutions.

CHAPTER 13: THE ART OF RESILIENCE

In the journey to success, resilience is your steadfast companion, the unwavering force that helps you weather life's storms and emerge stronger from adversity. Resilience is not a magical quality; it's a skill that can be developed and honed. This chapter delves into the art of resilience, exploring how to bounce back from setbacks, navigate challenges, and emerge triumphant.

Understanding Resilience

Resilience is the ability to adapt and thrive in the face of adversity, stress, or difficult situations. It's not about avoiding challenges but about developing the inner strength to confront and overcome them. Here's why resilience is a critical asset on your journey to success:

1. Empowerment in Adversity

Resilient individuals view challenges as opportunities for growth and learning. They embrace setbacks as stepping stones toward their goals.

2. Emotional Well-Being

Resilience is closely tied to emotional well-being. It enables you to manage stress, maintain a positive outlook, and bounce back from setbacks with grace.

3. Persistence

Resilience fuels persistence. It's the driving force that keeps you going when faced with obstacles and setbacks.

4. Improved Decision-Making

Resilient individuals make more rational and informed decisions, even in high-stress situations. They avoid impulsive reactions and consider the long-term consequences of their choices.

5. Stronger Relationships

Resilience fosters healthier relationships. It enables you to navigate conflicts and setbacks in relationships more effectively.

Building Resilience

Resilience is not a fixed trait but a skill that can be cultivated. Here are strategies to build and strengthen your resilience:

1. Develop a Growth Mindset

A growth mindset is the belief that your abilities and intelligence can be developed through effort and learning. Embrace challenges as opportunities to grow.

2. Cultivate Self-Awareness

Know your strengths and weaknesses. Self-awareness helps you recognize your emotional reactions and manage them effectively.

3. Establish a Support System

Connect with friends, family, or mentors who provide emotional support and guidance during tough times.

4. Practice Self-Care

Prioritize self-care activities that promote physical and mental well-being, such as exercise, meditation, and a balanced diet.

5. Set Realistic Goals

Set achievable, yet challenging, goals. Accomplishing these goals boosts your confidence and resilience.

6. Learn from Setbacks

Rather than dwelling on failures, analyze them for lessons. What can you learn from setbacks to improve your future endeavors?

Navigating Stress

Stress is an inevitable part of life, but how you respond to it can make a significant difference in your resilience. Here are strategies to navigate stress effectively:

1. Mindfulness and Relaxation Techniques

Practice mindfulness, meditation, or deep breathing exercises to calm your mind and reduce stress.

2. Time Management

Effective time management helps you balance your responsibilities and avoid overwhelming stress.

3. Seek Professional Help

If stress becomes overwhelming or leads to mental health challenges, don't hesitate to seek professional support.

Resilience in Action

As you continue on your path to success, you'll undoubtedly face challenges, setbacks, and unexpected twists. Resilience is your secret weapon, the inner strength that allows you to persevere and emerge stronger from these trials.

CHAPTER 14: THE POWER OF ADAPTABILITY

In the grand narrative of life, adaptability is the protagonist that enables you to navigate the ever-changing plot twists and turns. The ability to adapt is your secret weapon for success, helping you stay agile in a world that's in a constant state of flux. This chapter explores the art of adaptability, shedding light on how it can empower you to thrive amidst change and uncertainty.

Embracing Change as a Constant

Change is the one constant in life. From shifting career landscapes to evolving personal circumstances, it's inevitable. The ability to adapt not only eases the discomfort of change but also transforms it into a catalyst for growth. Here's why adaptability is essential on your journey to success:

1. Seizing Opportunities

Adaptability opens doors to new opportunities. It allows you to capitalize on unexpected turns of events and transform challenges into stepping stones.

2. Stress Reduction

When you embrace change rather than resist it, you reduce stress. Adaptability enables you to approach transitions with a sense of curiosity and readiness.

3. Enhanced Problem Solving

Adaptable individuals excel at problem-solving. They approach challenges with flexibility, exploring diverse solutions to find the most effective one.

4. Improved Resilience

Adaptability and resilience are intertwined. The ability to adapt builds your capacity to bounce back from setbacks and setbacks become mere detours rather than dead-ends.

The Components of Adaptability

Adaptability is more than just a mindset; it encompasses various elements that, when cultivated, empower you to thrive in a changing world:

1. Open-Mindedness

Be receptive to new ideas and perspectives. Approach change with a sense of curiosity rather than fear.

2. Flexibility

Adaptability requires flexibility in your thinking and actions. Be willing to adjust your plans and strategies as circumstances evolve.

3. Learning Orientation

View change as an opportunity to learn and grow. Seek out knowledge and new skills that can help you navigate transitions.

4. Emotional Regulation

Manage your emotions effectively when facing change. Emotionally intelligent adaptability is the ability to stay composed and make sound decisions amidst uncertainty.

5. Resilience

Resilience and adaptability are symbiotic. Resilience helps you persevere through change, and adaptability allows you to thrive in it.

Cultivating Adaptability

Adaptability is a skill you can nurture and develop. Here are strategies to cultivate adaptability in your life:

1. Embrace Change

Accept that change is a part of life. Rather than resisting it, approach it with an open mind and willingness to learn.

2. Emulate Role Models

Observe individuals who excel at adaptability. What strategies do they use? How do they approach change?

3. Step Out of Your Comfort Zone

Challenge yourself to try new things and take risks. Stepping out of your comfort zone fosters adaptability.

4. Seek Feedback

Regularly seek feedback from others to learn and grow. Constructive feedback helps you adapt and improve.

5. Build a Support Network

Surround yourself with a supportive network of friends, mentors, and colleagues who encourage your adaptability.

Adaptability in Action

As you continue your journey to success, remember that adaptability is your ally in a world characterized by constant change. Whether you're navigating career transitions, personal transformations, or unforeseen challenges, adaptability empowers you to not only survive but thrive amidst uncertainty.

CHAPTER 15: EFFECTIVE COMMUNICATION: THE KEYSTONE OF SUCCESS

Communication is the lifeblood of human interaction. It's the bridge that connects individuals, ideas, and aspirations. In your journey to success, mastering the art of effective communication is not a mere skill; it's a transformative superpower that can shape your destiny. This chapter dives into the profound impact of communication on your path to success, exploring its nuances, and providing practical strategies to become a skilled communicator.

The Power of Effective Communication

Effective communication is a multifaceted gem, offering a wealth of benefits for those who harness its potential. Here's why it's an indispensable asset on your journey to success:

1. Building Relationships

Communication is the cornerstone of healthy relationships, whether personal or professional. It fosters trust, understanding, and connection.

2. Conflict Resolution

Skilled communicators excel in resolving conflicts amicably. They navigate disagreements with empathy and find mutually beneficial solutions.

3. Leadership

Leadership hinges on communication. Inspirational leaders convey their vision, inspire action, and create a shared sense of purpose through effective communication.

4. Career Advancement

Communication prowess is often a differentiator in the workplace. It enhances your ability to influence, persuade, and lead others.

5. Personal Growth

Effective self-communication is the key to personal growth. It helps you set and achieve goals, manage emotions, and maintain a positive mindset.

Elements of Effective Communication

Effective communication goes beyond the mere exchange of words. It encompasses various elements that contribute to its success:

1. Listening Skills

Active listening is a cornerstone of effective communication. It involves not only hearing words but also understanding the underlying emotions and intentions.

2. Nonverbal Communication

Your body language, facial expressions, and gestures convey messages as powerful as words. Awareness of nonverbal cues enhances your communication.

3. Clarity and Conciseness

Effective communicators convey their message clearly and concisely. They eliminate ambiguity and ensure their audience understands their intent.

4. Empathy

Empathy is the ability to understand and share the feelings of others. It's the bedrock of effective interpersonal communication.

5. Adaptability

Adaptive communication involves tailoring your message to the needs and preferences of your audience. It ensures your message resonates with diverse individuals.

Cultivating Effective Communication

Effective communication is a skill that can be honed and refined over time. Here are strategies to cultivate and enhance your communication prowess:

1. Practice Active Listening

Develop active listening skills by giving your full attention to the speaker, asking clarifying questions, and validating their feelings.

2. Master Nonverbal Communication

Become aware of your own nonverbal cues and how they impact others. Practice open body language and use gestures intentionally.

3. Strive for Clarity

When communicating, prioritize clarity and simplicity. Use straightforward language and structure your message logically.

4. Cultivate Empathy

Empathize with others by seeking to understand their perspective and emotions. Validate their feelings and respond with compassion.

5. Adapt to Your Audience

Tailor your communication style to match the preferences and needs of your audience. Flexibility in your approach enhances your effectiveness.

Effective Communication in Action

As you continue your journey to success, remember that effective communication is your most potent tool for building bridges, inspiring action, and forging connections. Whether you're presenting to a room of colleagues, navigating personal relationships, or seeking to lead and influence, the ability to communicate effectively can make all the difference.

CHAPTER 16: THE ART OF PERSUASION

In the intricate tapestry of human interactions, persuasion is the thread that weaves influence and conviction. The ability to persuade is a valuable skill that transcends individual domains, from business and leadership to personal relationships and social impact. This chapter explores the art of persuasion, revealing its power and offering insights into becoming an effective persuader.

The Essence of Persuasion

Persuasion is the art of convincing others to adopt your viewpoint, support your ideas, or take a desired course of action. It's not about manipulation or coercion; it's about presenting your case in a compelling and ethical manner. Here's why persuasion is a critical tool on your journey to success:

1. Influence

Persuasion empowers you to influence the decisions and behaviors of others. It's a tool for creating change, rallying support, and inspiring action.

2. Leadership

Effective leaders are often skilled persuaders. They can articulate a vision, gain buy-in from their team, and inspire commitment to a common goal.

3. Negotiation

In negotiations, persuasion is a pivotal skill. It allows you to find mutually beneficial solutions, build consensus, and resolve conflicts.

4. Problem Solving

Persuasion is a tool for solving complex problems by aligning diverse perspectives and garnering support for innovative solutions.

5. Personal Growth

Persuasion is not limited to external interactions; it also applies to self-persuasion. It helps you motivate yourself to set and achieve ambitious goals.

The Art of Ethical Persuasion

Ethical persuasion is rooted in honesty, transparency, and respect for the autonomy of others. It's about presenting your case persuasively without resorting to deception or manipulation. Here are key principles of ethical persuasion:

1. Build Trust

Trust is the foundation of persuasion. Establish trust with your audience by being truthful, reliable, and genuine.

2. Understand Your Audience

Tailor your message to the needs, values, and interests of your audience. Effective persuasion begins with empathy and an understanding of your target's perspective.

3. Present Strong Evidence

Back your arguments with credible evidence, facts, and examples. Demonstrating the validity of your viewpoint enhances your persuasive impact.

4. Use Persuasive Techniques

Utilize persuasion techniques such as storytelling, social proof, and appealing to emotions to make your case more compelling.

5. Respect Autonomy

Respect the autonomy of your audience. Allow them the freedom to make their own decisions, even if it differs from your desired outcome.

Cultivating Persuasive Skills

Persuasion is a skill that can be cultivated and enhanced. Here are strategies to become a more persuasive communicator:

1. Hone Your Communication Skills

Effective communication is the bedrock of persuasion. Work on your listening, speaking, and nonverbal communication skills.

2. Practice Empathy

Empathize with your audience to understand their needs, concerns, and motivations. Tailor your message accordingly.

3. Develop Confidence

Confidence in your message and your ability to present it persuasively is essential. Practice and preparation boost confidence.

4. Study Persuasive Techniques

Learn about different persuasion techniques and apply them judiciously in your communication.

5. Seek Feedback

Gather feedback from others to evaluate the effectiveness of your persuasive efforts. Continuous improvement is key.

Persuasion in Action

As you continue your journey to success, remember that persuasion is not about manipulating or coercing others but about building consensus and inspiring action. Whether you're seeking to advance your career, rally support for a cause, or win over a skeptical audience, the art of persuasion can be your guiding star.

CHAPTER 17: THE ART OF DECISION-MAKING

Decisions are the building blocks of our lives. They shape our destinies, influence our outcomes, and define our paths to success. The art of decision-making is not just about choosing between options; it's about making informed, effective choices that propel you toward your goals. In this chapter, we will delve into the intricacies of decision-making, exploring the psychology behind it and offering strategies to become a more adept decision-maker.

The Significance of Decision-Making

Every day, we make countless decisions, from what to wear to life-altering choices in our careers and relationships. Here's why mastering the art of decision-making is crucial on your journey to success:

1. Impact on Success

The quality of your decisions directly impacts your success. Wise choices can lead to favorable outcomes, while poor decisions can hinder progress.

2. Confidence and Clarity

Effective decision-making fosters confidence and clarity. It empowers you to navigate uncertainty with poise.

3. Adaptability

The ability to make quick, well-informed decisions is a hallmark of adaptability, a valuable skill in our dynamic world.

4. Problem Solving

Decision-making is a form of problem-solving. It involves identifying challenges, evaluating options, and selecting the best course of action.

5. Personal Growth

Your decisions shape your personal growth. The choices you make influence your learning experiences, values, and character development.

The Decision-Making Process

Effective decision-making is a structured process that involves several key steps. Let's explore the decision-making process:

1. Define the Problem

Begin by clearly defining the problem or decision you need to make. What is the issue, and what are your goals?

2. Gather Information

Collect relevant information and data. Seek out facts, opinions, and insights to inform your decision.

3. Generate Options

Brainstorm potential solutions or courses of action. Encourage creativity and consider various possibilities.

4. Evaluate Options

Assess each option based on criteria such as feasibility, impact, and alignment with your goals and values.

5. Make the Decision

Choose the option that best meets your criteria and aligns with your objectives. Trust your judgment and make the decision confidently.

6. Implement the Decision

Put your decision into action. Develop a plan and execute it effectively.

7. Review and Learn

After implementing your decision, evaluate the results. What worked well, and what could be improved? Use this feedback to inform future decisions.

Overcoming Decision-Making Challenges

Effective decision-making can be challenging, and we often encounter obstacles along the way. Here are strategies to overcome common decision-making challenges:

1. Avoid Decision Paralysis

When faced with too many choices, simplify your options by focusing on what truly matters. Identify your core criteria and use them to filter choices.

2. Manage Emotions

Emotions can cloud judgment. Take a step back and consider your decision objectively, weighing both rational and emotional factors.

3. Seek Advice

Don't hesitate to seek advice from trusted mentors, friends, or experts. Different perspectives can provide valuable insights.

4. Embrace Uncertainty

Accept that some level of uncertainty is inherent in decision-making. Make the best choice based on available information, knowing that perfect certainty is rare.

5. Learn from Mistakes

Don't fear making mistakes. Mistakes are opportunities for learning and growth. Analyze them to make better decisions in the future.

Decision-Making in Action

As you continue your journey to success, remember that every decision you make shapes your path. Whether you're making choices about your career, relationships, or personal development, the art of decision-making is your compass. It guides you toward the destinations you desire.

CHAPTER 18: THE MASTERY OF TIME MANAGEMENT

Time is our most finite resource. It's the currency of life, and how we invest it profoundly impacts our journey to success. The art of time management isn't about doing more; it's about doing what truly matters. In this chapter, we will explore the art of mastering time, uncovering strategies to optimize your days, increase productivity, and create a harmonious work-life balance.

The Value of Time

Time is the great equalizer. Regardless of your background or circumstances, you have the same 24 hours in a day. Here's why effective time management is a linchpin on your path to success:

1. Productivity

Effective time management enhances productivity. It empowers you to accomplish more in less time, leaving room for creative pursuits and personal growth.

2. Focus and Clarity

Time management sharpens your focus and clarity. It helps you prioritize tasks and eliminate distractions.

3. Goal Achievement

Time management aligns your actions with your goals. It ensures that you allocate time to the activities that contribute most to your success.

4. Stress Reduction

Properly managed time reduces stress. It prevents the rush and panic of last-minute deadlines and fosters a sense of control.

5. Work-Life Balance

Time management enables you to strike a healthy work-life balance. It allows you to allocate time not just for work but also for personal well-being, relationships, and leisure.

The Time Management Spectrum

Time management techniques vary widely, and what works best for one person may not work for another. Here are key approaches to time management:

1. Prioritization

Identify your most important tasks and allocate time to them. Prioritization ensures that you focus on activities that align with your goals.

2. Time Blocking

Time blocking involves scheduling specific blocks of time for tasks and activities. It provides structure and prevents multitasking.

3. To-Do Lists

Create to-do lists to organize your tasks and track progress. Lists help you stay on top of deadlines and commitments.

4. The Two-Minute Rule

If a task can be completed in two minutes or less, do it immediately. This rule prevents small tasks from piling up.

5. Digital Tools

Use digital tools and apps to manage your time efficiently. Calendar apps, task managers, and project management software can streamline your workflow.

Overcoming Time Management Challenges

Effective time management can be challenging in a world filled with distractions and demands. Here are strategies to overcome common time management challenges:

1. Set Boundaries

Establish boundaries to protect your time. Say no to non-essential commitments and learn to decline requests that don't align with your priorities.

2. Eliminate Time Wasters

Identify and eliminate time-wasting habits, such as excessive social media use or unproductive meetings.

3. Delegate Tasks

Delegate tasks when possible. Trust others to share the workload and free up your time for more high-impact activities.

4. Take Breaks

Schedule regular breaks to recharge. Short breaks can improve focus and overall productivity.

5. Reflect and Adjust

Regularly evaluate your time management strategies. Adjust your approach based on what works best for you and your evolving priorities.

Time Management in Action

As you continue your journey to success, remember that time

is your most valuable asset. Effective time management is not just about doing more; it's about doing what matters most. Whether you're pursuing a career goal, nurturing relationships, or seeking personal growth, the art of time management is your compass.

CHAPTER 19: THE ART OF RESILIENCE

Resilience is the ability to bounce back from adversity, to weather life's storms with grace and determination. It's not just about surviving; it's about thriving in the face of challenges. In this chapter, we will delve into the art of resilience, exploring what it means to be resilient, why it's crucial on your journey to success, and how to cultivate this invaluable quality.

Understanding Resilience

Resilience is not a fixed trait; it's a dynamic skill that can be developed and strengthened. It involves adaptability, mental toughness, and the ability to maintain a positive outlook during tough times. Here's why resilience is vital on your path to success:

1. Embracing Change

Life is filled with unexpected twists and turns. Resilience helps you adapt to change and find opportunities within adversity.

2. Overcoming Setbacks

Success often involves setbacks and failures. Resilience empowers you to bounce back from disappointments and keep moving forward.

3. Handling Stress

Resilient individuals are better equipped to manage stress and maintain their emotional well-being.

4. Navigating Uncertainty

In an unpredictable world, resilience provides a steady compass. It helps you stay focused on your goals despite uncertainty.

5. Building Confidence

Overcoming challenges boosts confidence. Resilience enables you to tackle bigger challenges with self-assurance.

The Elements of Resilience

Resilience encompasses various elements that contribute to its development. Here are key components of resilience:

1. Self-Awareness

Self-awareness involves recognizing your emotions, thoughts, and reactions. It's the first step toward building resilience.

2. Positive Mindset

A positive mindset doesn't ignore challenges but rather focuses on solutions and opportunities. It's the foundation of resilience.

3. Problem-Solving Skills

Resilient individuals are adept problem solvers. They approach challenges with a solution-oriented mindset.

4. Social Support

Having a network of supportive friends, family, or mentors is crucial for resilience. Social connections provide emotional strength during tough times.

5. Adaptability

Resilience requires adaptability—the ability to adjust your strategies and perspectives when faced with adversity.

Cultivating Resilience

Resilience is a skill that can be nurtured and strengthened over time. Here are strategies to cultivate resilience in your life:

1. Develop Self-Awareness

Start by developing self-awareness. Reflect on your emotions and reactions, and learn to manage them effectively.

2. Practice Optimism

Cultivate a positive outlook. Focus on solutions, find silver linings in challenges, and maintain hope for the future.

3. Build Strong Connections

Nurture your social support network. Connect with people who uplift and encourage you during tough times.

4. Develop Problem-Solving Skills

Enhance your problem-solving skills. Break challenges into manageable steps and approach them with a clear plan.

5. Embrace Change

Embrace change as an opportunity for growth. Be open to new experiences and challenges that push you outside your comfort zone.

Resilience in Action

As you continue your journey to success, remember that resilience is your secret weapon against adversity. It's the ability to rise stronger after every fall, to adapt, and to keep moving toward your goals despite obstacles.

CHAPTER 20: THE ART OF CONTINUOUS LEARNING

Learning is not confined to the walls of a classroom or the pages of a textbook. It's a lifelong journey, an art that, when mastered, becomes a powerful force propelling you toward success. In this chapter, we will delve into the art of continuous learning, exploring why it's essential, how it shapes your path, and practical strategies to become an avid, perpetual learner.

The Lifelong Pursuit of Knowledge

The pursuit of knowledge doesn't have an expiration date. It's not reserved for formal education but is a continuous, enriching process that unfolds throughout your life. Here's why continuous learning is vital on your journey to success:

1. Adaptability

In our rapidly changing world, adaptability is key. Continuous learning ensures you remain agile, ready to embrace new technologies and navigate evolving landscapes.

2. Innovation

Learning fuels innovation. New ideas and breakthroughs often emerge from a foundation of knowledge and a curious mind.

3. Career Advancement

In your career, continuous learning sets you apart. It equips you with the skills and expertise needed to excel in your field and seize new opportunities.

4. Personal Growth

Learning is a gateway to personal growth. It broadens your horizons, deepens your understanding of the world, and fosters self-discovery.

5. Problem Solving

Continuous learning sharpens your problem-solving skills. It empowers you to tackle complex challenges with creativity and insight.

The Art of Lifelong Learning

Lifelong learning is more than just acquiring facts; it's about developing a mindset and habits that nurture your curiosity and thirst for knowledge. Here are key elements of this art:

1. Curiosity

Embrace curiosity as your driving force. Ask questions, seek answers, and explore topics that pique your interest.

2. Open-Mindedness

Be open to diverse perspectives and ideas. Recognize that learning often involves unlearning and relearning.

3. Self-Directed Learning

Take charge of your learning journey. Set goals, seek out resources, and create a personal learning plan.

4. Critical Thinking

Develop critical thinking skills. Analyze information, evaluate sources, and discern between reliable and unreliable information.

5. Continuous Exploration

Don't limit your learning to your comfort zone. Explore new subjects, cultures, and experiences to expand your horizons.

Cultivating a Learning Lifestyle

Becoming a lifelong learner is a transformative lifestyle choice. Here are strategies to cultivate a culture of continuous learning in your life:

1. Set Learning Goals

Define what you want to learn and why. Set specific goals that guide your learning journey.

2. Create a Learning Routine

Establish a regular learning routine. Dedicate time each day or week to acquiring new knowledge or skills.

3. Diversify Resources

Explore various learning resources, from books and courses to podcasts, workshops, and online communities.

4. Engage in Discussions

Engage in discussions and debates about what you've learned. Sharing knowledge with others deepens your understanding.

5. Embrace Failure

Don't fear making mistakes or encountering challenges in your learning journey. Embrace failure as an opportunity to grow.

Learning in Action

As you continue your journey to success, remember that the path is paved with opportunities to learn and grow. Lifelong learning isn't just a skill; it's a way of life that enriches your experience and expands your horizons.

CHAPTER 21: THE POWER OF NETWORKING

Success is seldom a solitary journey. It thrives on connections—with people, opportunities, and ideas. In this chapter, we will delve into the power of networking, exploring why it's essential, how it influences your path to success, and practical strategies to build meaningful, lasting connections in both personal and professional spheres.

The Network of Success

Your network isn't just a list of contacts; it's a web of relationships that can open doors, provide support, and amplify your potential. Here's why networking is crucial on your journey to success:

1. Opportunities

Networking exposes you to a world of opportunities. It can lead to job offers, collaborations, mentorships, and new ventures.

2. Knowledge Exchange

Through networking, you can tap into the wisdom and experiences of others. It's a two-way street where you both learn and share insights.

3. Support System

A robust network provides a support system during challenging times. It's a source of encouragement, advice, and emotional backing.

4. Visibility

Networking enhances your visibility in your field or industry. It can help you stand out and be recognized for your expertise.

5. Personal Growth

Interacting with diverse individuals and perspectives fosters personal growth. It broadens your horizons and enriches your worldview.

Building Meaningful Connections

Effective networking isn't about collecting business cards; it's about cultivating meaningful, mutually beneficial relationships. Here are key principles of building a strong network:

1. Authenticity

Be yourself in your interactions. Authenticity builds trust and lasting connections.

2. Give Before You Receive

Don't approach networking with a "what's in it for me" mindset. Be generous with your knowledge, time, and resources.

3. Listen Actively

Effective networking involves active listening. Show genuine interest in others, and ask questions that demonstrate your curiosity.

4. Be Consistent

Nurture your network consistently, not just when you need something. Regular communication maintains relationships.

5. Diversify Your Network

Expand your network beyond your immediate field. Diversity of thought and background can spark new ideas and opportunities.

Strategies for Effective Networking

Building a network takes time and effort. Here are strategies to enhance your networking skills:

1. Attend Events

Participate in industry conferences, seminars, and local meetups. These events provide opportunities to meet like-minded individuals.

2. Join Professional Organizations

Become a member of professional organizations related to your field. These groups often host networking events and offer resources for career development.

3. Utilize Social Media

Leverage social media platforms like LinkedIn to connect with professionals in your industry. Share your insights and engage in discussions.

4. Volunteer

Volunteer for causes or organizations you are passionate about. It's a great way to meet people who share your values.

5. Seek Mentors and Advisors

Look for mentors and advisors who can guide you in your career. Their wisdom and connections can be invaluable.

Networking in Action

As you continue your journey to success, remember that your network is a dynamic, evolving asset. It's not just a collection of names but a source of inspiration, support, and opportunities.

CHAPTER 22: THE ART OF PUBLIC SPEAKING

Public speaking is a skill that transcends the podium. It's a tool for conveying ideas, inspiring change, and connecting with others on a profound level. In this chapter, we will explore the art of public speaking, uncovering why it's essential, how it shapes your journey to success, and practical strategies to become an effective communicator, whether addressing a room full of people or having a one-on-one conversation.

The Power of Effective Communication

Effective communication is the cornerstone of personal and professional success. It's not just about talking; it's about conveying ideas, building connections, and inspiring action. Here's why public speaking is crucial on your path to success:

1. Influence

Public speaking allows you to influence and persuade others. Whether you're presenting a proposal at work or advocating for a cause, the ability to articulate your message persuasively is invaluable.

2. Leadership

Leaders are often defined by their ability to communicate a compelling vision. Public speaking is a leadership skill that empowers you to inspire and guide others.

3. Connection

Great speakers connect with their audience on an emotional level. Effective communication fosters understanding and empathy, strengthening relationships.

4. Career Advancement

The ability to speak confidently and convincingly can fast-track your career. It positions you as a thought leader and opens doors to new opportunities.

5. Self-Expression

Public speaking is a means of self-expression. It empowers you to share your thoughts, experiences, and expertise with the world.

Becoming an Effective Speaker

Public speaking isn't reserved for a select few; it's a skill that can be honed and refined. Here are key elements of becoming an effective speaker:

1. Confidence

Confidence is the foundation of effective public speaking. Believe in your message and your ability to convey it.

2. Clarity

Be clear and concise in your communication. Organize your thoughts logically and avoid jargon or unnecessary complexity.

3. Engagement

Engage your audience by telling stories, asking questions, or using visual aids. Make your message relatable and memorable.

4. Practice

Practice is essential for improvement. Rehearse your speech multiple times, focusing on both content and delivery.

5. Feedback

Seek feedback from trusted sources. Constructive criticism can help you refine your speaking skills.

Strategies for Effective Public Speaking

Becoming an effective public speaker requires practice and dedication. Here are strategies to enhance your public speaking abilities:

1. Know Your Audience

Understand your audience's needs, interests, and expectations. Tailor your message to resonate with them.

2. Master Nonverbal Communication

Pay attention to your body language, tone of voice, and facial expressions. Nonverbal cues can greatly impact how your message is received.

3. Use Visual Aids Wisely

If using visual aids, ensure they enhance your message rather than distract from it. Keep slides simple and uncluttered.

4. Manage Nervousness

Nervousness is common, even among seasoned speakers. Channel nervous energy into enthusiasm and practice relaxation techniques.

5. Record and Reflect

Record your speeches and review them for areas of improvement. Reflect on what worked well and what could be enhanced.

Public Speaking in Action

As you continue your journey to success, remember that public speaking is a skill that can be developed over time. It's a powerful tool for conveying your ideas, inspiring change, and connecting with others on a profound level.

CHAPTER 23: THE ART OF TIME MANAGEMENT

Time is the most precious resource we possess, yet it often slips through our fingers unnoticed. The art of time management is a critical skill on your journey to success. In this chapter, we will explore why effective time management is essential, how it influences your path, and practical strategies to maximize your productivity, prioritize tasks, and make the most of each day.

The Value of Time

Time is a finite resource, and how you use it directly impacts your personal and professional success. Here's why effective time management is crucial:

1. Productivity

Time management enhances your productivity. It enables you to accomplish more in less time, freeing up space for new endeavors.

2. Goal Achievement

Successful individuals recognize the importance of aligning their time with their goals. Time management ensures you stay on track.

3. Reduced Stress

Properly managed time reduces stress. It helps you meet deadlines, avoid last-minute rushes, and maintain work-life balance.

4. Opportunity Maximization

Effective time management allows you to seize opportunities when they arise. It ensures you're prepared to make the most of serendipitous moments.

5. Quality of Life

Balancing work and personal time is vital for a fulfilling life. Time management helps you prioritize what truly matters.

Mastering Time Management

Time management isn't about squeezing every second out of your day but rather optimizing your time for meaningful pursuits. Here are key elements of mastering time management:

1. Goal Setting

Start by setting clear, achievable goals. Your goals provide direction for how you allocate your time.

2. Prioritization

Not all tasks are equal. Prioritize your tasks based on importance and deadlines. Focus on high-impact activities.

3. Time Blocking

Use time blocking to schedule specific periods for different tasks. This technique minimizes distractions and increases focus.

4. Delegation

Recognize that you can't do everything yourself. Delegate tasks when possible to free up your time for higher-priority activities.

5. Efficient Workflows

Streamline your workflows. Look for ways to automate repetitive tasks and eliminate time-wasting habits.

Strategies for Effective Time Management

Effective time management is a skill that can be cultivated. Here are strategies to enhance your time management abilities:

1. Create a To-Do List

Start your day by creating a to-do list. List tasks in order of priority to guide your focus.

2. Set Time Limits

Allocate specific time limits to tasks. Knowing you have a limited time frame can boost productivity.

3. Minimize Multitasking

While multitasking may seem efficient, it often leads to lower quality work. Focus on one task at a time.

4. Learn to Say No

Don't overcommit. Learn to say no to tasks or projects that don't align with your goals or available time.

5. Regularly Review and Adjust

Periodically review your time management strategies. Adjust as needed to optimize your efficiency.

Time Management in Action

As you continue your journey to success, remember that time management is a dynamic process. It's about making deliberate choices about how you spend your time to align with your goals and priorities.

CHAPTER 24: THE ART OF DECISION-MAKING

Life is a series of decisions, both big and small. Every choice you make shapes your path and influences your journey to success. In this chapter, we will explore the art of decision-making, uncovering why it's essential, how it impacts your life, and practical strategies to make sound, effective decisions that align with your goals and values.

The Role of Decision-Making

Decision-making is at the heart of every endeavor, from choosing a career path to deciding what to have for breakfast. Here's why effective decision-making is crucial:

1. Impact

Decisions have consequences. The choices you make can have a profound impact on your personal and professional life.

2. Goal Achievement

Effective decision-making is essential for reaching your goals. Decisions should align with your aspirations and priorities.

3. Adaptability

In an ever-changing world, the ability to make informed, adaptive decisions is a valuable skill. It enables you to navigate uncertainty and seize opportunities.

4. Problem Solving

Decision-making is problem-solving in action. It's about identifying challenges, evaluating options, and choosing the best course of action.

5. Confidence

Mastering the art of decision-making boosts your confidence. It empowers you to trust your judgment and take calculated risks.

The Art of Effective Decision-Making

Effective decision-making isn't about always being right; it's about making thoughtful, informed choices. Here are key elements of the art of decision-making:

1. Clarity of Purpose

Start with a clear understanding of your goals and values. Knowing what you aim to achieve provides a foundation for your decisions.

2. Information Gathering

Collect relevant information before making a decision. Research, seek advice, and consider various perspectives.

3. Analytical Thinking

Use analytical thinking to evaluate options. Consider the pros and cons, potential risks, and long-term consequences.

4. Gut Feeling

Trust your intuition. Sometimes, your gut feeling can provide valuable insights when making decisions.

5. Learn from Mistakes

Embrace the possibility of making mistakes. Every decision, whether successful or not, offers lessons for future choices.

Strategies for Effective Decision-Making

Effective decision-making is a skill you can develop and refine. Here are strategies to enhance your decision-making abilities:

1. Avoid Decision Fatigue

Limit the number of decisions you make in a day. Trivial choices can deplete your mental energy.

2. Set Decision-Making Criteria

Define criteria that align with your goals. Use these criteria as a framework for evaluating options.

3. Seek Feedback

Consult with trusted individuals who can provide valuable insights and perspectives on your decisions.

4. Break Down Complex Decisions

For complex decisions, break them down into smaller, manageable steps. This simplifies the process and reduces overwhelm.

5. Reflect on Past Decisions

Review your past decisions, both successful and unsuccessful. Reflect on what you've learned from each experience.

Decision-Making in Action

As you continue your journey to success, remember that every decision is a step forward. Whether you're choosing a career, making financial investments, or deciding on personal matters, the art of decision-making is your compass.

CHAPTER 25: THE POWER OF NETWORKING

Success rarely happens in isolation. It's often the result of connections, collaborations, and relationships built over time. In this chapter, we will explore the power of networking, uncovering why it's a critical element of your journey to success, how it shapes your opportunities, and practical strategies to expand your network and make meaningful connections.

The Significance of Networking

Networking is more than just attending social events or collecting business cards. It's about building genuine relationships with others who share your interests or goals. Here's why networking is essential:

1. Opportunity Creation

Networking opens doors to new opportunities. Whether it's finding a job, launching a business, or discovering a mentor, your network can provide valuable leads.

2. Knowledge Exchange

Interacting with diverse individuals allows you to gain insights and knowledge from different perspectives. It broadens your understanding of various industries and fields.

3. Support System

Your network can be a source of support during challenging times. Whether you need advice, encouragement, or assistance, your connections can provide it.

4. Collaboration

Collaboration often leads to innovation and growth. Networking introduces you to potential collaborators who can help you achieve your goals.

5. Personal Development

Networking is a means of personal growth. It enhances your communication skills, adaptability, and ability to connect with people from diverse backgrounds.

The Art of Effective Networking

Effective networking isn't about quantity; it's about quality. Building authentic connections is key. Here are key elements of effective networking:

1. Genuine Interest

Approach networking with a genuine interest in others. Listen actively and ask questions to get to know people on a deeper level.

2. Reciprocity

Networking is a two-way street. Offer your assistance and support to others, and they are likely to reciprocate.

3. Consistency

Consistency is essential in networking. Regularly engage with your connections to maintain and strengthen relationships.

4. Diverse Network

Seek diversity in your network. Connect with individuals from various backgrounds, industries, and experiences.

5. Follow-Up

After initial contact, follow up with your connections. Send a thank-you message or an update on your progress. Keeping in touch reinforces your relationship.

Strategies for Effective Networking

Effective networking is a skill you can develop and refine. Here are strategies to enhance your networking abilities:

1. Attend Networking Events

Attend conferences, seminars, workshops, and social gatherings related to your field or interests. These events are ideal for meeting like-minded individuals.

2. Use Online Platforms

Leverage online platforms like LinkedIn to expand your professional network. Connect with people in your industry and engage in discussions.

3. Join Clubs or Groups

Participate in clubs, organizations, or online groups that align with your hobbies or passions. This can lead to meaningful connections with shared interests.

4. Seek Mentorship

Find a mentor in your field who can provide guidance and support. Mentorship is a valuable aspect of networking.

5. Give Before You Receive

Be willing to help others before seeking assistance. Offering your knowledge or assistance builds goodwill in your network.

Networking in Action

As you continue your journey to success, remember that

networking is more than a business transaction. It's about building relationships with individuals who can enrich your life both professionally and personally.

CHAPTER 26: THE POWER OF RESILIENCE

Life is full of ups and downs, and your journey to success is no exception. In this chapter, we'll delve into the power of resilience, exploring why it's a crucial trait, how it influences your path, and practical strategies to cultivate resilience in the face of challenges and setbacks.

The Importance of Resilience

Resilience is your ability to bounce back from adversity, adapt to change, and keep moving forward. Here's why resilience is vital:

1. Overcoming Setbacks

In your pursuit of success, you will inevitably face setbacks and failures. Resilience allows you to view these as opportunities for growth rather than roadblocks.

2. Embracing Change

The world is constantly changing, and adaptability is a valuable skill. Resilience enables you to navigate change with grace and optimism.

3. Mental Well-Being

Resilience is closely tied to mental well-being. It helps you manage stress, anxiety, and depression more effectively.

4. Long-Term Goals

Success often requires long-term commitment. Resilience keeps you focused and determined, even when the path is challenging.

5. Empowerment

Resilience empowers you to take charge of your circumstances. It shifts your mindset from victimhood to agency.

Cultivating Resilience

Resilience is not a fixed trait; it's a skill that can be developed and strengthened. Here are key elements of cultivating resilience:

1. Positive Mindset

Maintain a positive outlook, even in difficult times. Focus on solutions and opportunities rather than dwelling on problems.

2. Emotional Regulation

Learn to manage your emotions effectively. Practices like mindfulness and meditation can help you stay calm and centered.

3. Problem-Solving

Develop strong problem-solving skills. Break challenges into smaller, manageable steps and tackle them systematically.

4. Social Support

Lean on your social network for support. Friends, family, and mentors can provide valuable encouragement and guidance.

5. Self-Care

Prioritize self-care to boost your physical and mental resilience. Exercise, a balanced diet, and sufficient sleep are essential.

Strategies for Building Resilience

Building resilience is an ongoing process. Here are strategies to enhance your resilience:

1. Set Realistic Goals

Set achievable goals that challenge you without overwhelming you. This allows you to experience small victories along the way.

2. Cultivate Adaptability

Embrace change as an opportunity for growth. Seek out new experiences and challenges that push you out of your comfort zone.

3. Learn from Failure

Instead of fearing failure, view it as a stepping stone to success. Analyze what went wrong and how you can improve.

4. Build a Support Network

Surround yourself with people who uplift and support you. These connections can provide a safety net during tough times.

5. Practice Gratitude

Regularly express gratitude for the positive aspects of your life. This fosters a positive mindset.

Resilience in Action

As you continue your journey to success, remember that resilience is your ally in navigating the inevitable obstacles and setbacks. It's not about avoiding challenges but about facing them with strength and determination.

CHAPTER 27: THE SCIENCE OF PRODUCTIVITY

Productivity is the engine that drives progress, both in our personal lives and professional endeavors. In this chapter, we will explore the science of productivity, uncovering the psychological and practical aspects that can help you enhance your efficiency, accomplish more, and ultimately achieve your goals.

Understanding Productivity

Productivity is often associated with how much work you can accomplish in a given amount of time. However, it's more complex than simply getting more done. True productivity involves doing meaningful work efficiently and effectively. Here's why productivity matters:

1. Goal Achievement

Being productive allows you to make steady progress toward your goals. Whether it's completing a project, launching a business, or achieving a personal milestone, productivity is the key to success.

2. Time Management

Productivity is closely linked to time management. By maximizing your productivity, you can make the most of your available time and avoid wasting precious hours on unimportant tasks.

3. Reduced Stress

When you're productive, you're more likely to stay on top of your tasks and deadlines, reducing stress and anxiety related to unfinished work.

4. Self-Efficacy

Accomplishing tasks and projects boosts your self-esteem and confidence. This sense of self-efficacy can have a positive impact on various aspects of your life.

The Science Behind Productivity

Understanding the science of productivity can help you harness your full potential. Here are some key psychological aspects of productivity:

1. Motivation

Motivation is a critical driver of productivity. It's the inner force that compels you to start and finish tasks. Identifying your sources of motivation can help you stay productive.

2. Focus and Attention

Productivity requires sustained focus and attention. Minimizing distractions, setting clear goals, and practicing mindfulness can enhance your ability to concentrate.

3. Time Management

Effective time management involves prioritization and planning. Tools like the Eisenhower Matrix and the Pomodoro Technique can help you allocate your time wisely.

4. Goal Setting

Setting SMART (Specific, Measurable, Achievable, Relevant,

Time-bound) goals provides a clear roadmap for your productivity efforts. It gives you a sense of direction and purpose.

Practical Strategies for Boosting Productivity

While understanding the psychological aspects of productivity is essential, practical strategies are equally important. Here are some strategies to enhance your productivity:

1. Prioritize Tasks

Identify your most important tasks (MITs) each day and tackle them first. This ensures that you're working on high-impact activities.

2. Time Blocking

Allocate specific blocks of time to work on particular tasks or projects. This minimizes multitasking and increases focus.

3. Break Tasks into Smaller Steps

Breaking tasks into smaller, more manageable steps makes them less daunting and easier to complete.

4. Set Deadlines

Establish self-imposed deadlines for tasks. A sense of urgency can boost your productivity.

5. Take Breaks

Regular breaks, especially short, frequent ones, can recharge your energy and improve your overall productivity.

6. Stay Organized

Maintain an organized workspace and digital environment. Clutter can be distracting and hinder your productivity.

Productivity in Action

As you continue your journey to success, remember that productivity is not a one-size-fits-all concept. What works for one person may not work for another. It's about finding the strategies and techniques that align with your unique preferences and needs.

CHAPTER 28: THE ART OF DECISION-MAKING

Every day, we make countless decisions that shape our lives, from the trivial choices of what to eat for breakfast to life-altering decisions like changing careers or starting a family. In this chapter, we will delve into the art of decision-making, uncovering the psychology behind it, the factors that influence our choices, and practical strategies to make better decisions.

The Significance of Decision-Making

Decision-making is a fundamental aspect of human existence. It plays a pivotal role in our personal and professional lives, often determining our success, happiness, and overall well-being. Here's why decision-making matters:

1. Life Direction

Major decisions, such as choosing a career or life partner, shape the course of your life. They define your trajectory and long-term goals.

2. Problem Solving

Decision-making is problem-solving in action. It's how you tackle challenges, address issues, and find solutions to complex situations.

3. Risk Management

Every decision involves a level of risk. Effective decision-making helps you assess and manage risks, enabling you to make informed choices.

4. Self-Expression

Your choices are a form of self-expression. They reflect your values, priorities, and beliefs to the world.

The Psychology of Decision-Making

Understanding the psychology behind decision-making can shed light on why we make certain choices. Here are some key psychological factors:

1. Cognitive Biases

Cognitive biases are mental shortcuts that influence our decisions. Common biases like confirmation bias and availability heuristic can lead to flawed choices.

2. Emotions

Emotions play a significant role in decision-making. They can cloud judgment or provide valuable insights, depending on how they are managed.

3. Rationality and Intuition

Decisions can be made through rational analysis or intuitive gut feelings. Balancing both approaches can lead to well-rounded choices.

4. Prospect Theory

Prospect theory suggests that people are more sensitive to potential losses than gains. This can impact risk aversion and choices related to loss avoidance.

Strategies for Effective Decision-Making

Making better decisions is a skill that can be honed. Here are strategies to enhance your decision-making abilities:

1. Gather Information

Before making a decision, collect as much relevant information as possible. This ensures your choices are based on a solid foundation.

2. Define Objectives

Clearly define your objectives and priorities. What do you want to achieve with this decision? Having a clear goal guides your choice.

3. Weigh Pros and Cons

List the pros and cons of each option. This helps you visualize the potential outcomes and trade-offs.

4. Consider Alternatives

Explore different alternatives and solutions. Don't limit yourself to the first options that come to mind.

5. Seek Advice

Consult with trusted friends, mentors, or experts when facing significant decisions. External perspectives can provide valuable insights.

6. Manage Emotions

Recognize and manage your emotions during the decision-making process. Emotional decisions can lead to regrets, so strive for a balanced approach.

7. Set a Time Frame

Decisions should have a time frame. Avoid procrastinating or rushing decisions when unnecessary.

Decision-Making in Action

As you continue your journey to success, remember that every choice you make has consequences. By mastering the art of decision-making, you empower yourself to navigate life's complexities with confidence and clarity.

CHAPTER 29: THE POWER OF RESILIENCE

Resilience is a remarkable quality that empowers individuals to bounce back from adversity, challenges, and setbacks. It's the ability to withstand the storms of life and emerge stronger than before. In this chapter, we will explore the profound significance of resilience, its psychological underpinnings, and practical strategies to cultivate and harness this invaluable trait.

The Essence of Resilience

Resilience is not merely about enduring difficulties; it's about thriving in the face of them. Resilient individuals possess an unwavering determination to overcome obstacles and setbacks, using them as stepping stones toward growth and personal development. Here's why resilience is crucial:

1. Adapting to Change

Life is full of change, both expected and unexpected. Resilience equips you with the flexibility and adaptability needed to navigate transitions smoothly.

2. Building Confidence

Overcoming challenges boosts self-confidence. Each success in the face of adversity reinforces your belief in your abilities.

3. Emotional Well-Being

Resilience contributes to emotional well-being by helping you manage stress, anxiety, and depression. It fosters a positive outlook on life.

4. Achieving Goals

Resilience is the driving force behind goal achievement. When setbacks occur, resilient individuals don't abandon their objectives; they adjust their strategies and persevere.

The Psychology of Resilience

Understanding the psychology behind resilience provides insight into how it can be developed and nurtured. Here are some key psychological components of resilience:

1. Optimism

Optimism is the belief that challenges can be overcome and that positive outcomes are possible. Cultivating a sense of optimism is central to resilience.

2. Emotional Regulation

Resilient individuals are skilled at managing their emotions. They acknowledge their feelings without being overwhelmed by them, enabling them to make rational decisions.

3. Problem-Solving Skills

Resilience involves effective problem-solving. It's about finding solutions rather than dwelling on problems.

4. Social Support

A strong support network is a key element of resilience. Friends, family, and mentors provide encouragement and assistance during tough times.

Strategies for Cultivating Resilience

Resilience is a quality that can be developed and strengthened over time. Here are strategies to enhance your resilience:

1. Develop a Growth Mindset

Embrace challenges as opportunities for growth. Adopt a mindset that sees setbacks as a chance to learn and improve.

2. Build a Support System

Cultivate strong relationships with people who provide emotional support and guidance. Lean on your support network during challenging times.

3. Self-Care

Take care of your physical and mental health. A healthy body and mind are better equipped to handle adversity.

4. Practice Mindfulness

Mindfulness techniques, such as meditation and deep breathing, can help you stay grounded and calm in the face of stress.

5. Set Realistic Goals

Set achievable goals and break them into smaller, manageable steps. This prevents feeling overwhelmed and boosts your sense of accomplishment.

6. Learn from Setbacks

When setbacks occur, take time to reflect on what went wrong and what you can learn from the experience. Use this knowledge to improve.

Resilience in Action

As you continue your journey toward success, remember that resilience is your ally when facing the inevitable challenges and setbacks that lie ahead. It's the inner strength that propels you forward when the path is unclear and the storms are fierce.

CHAPTER 30: THE SCIENCE OF CREATIVITY

Creativity is a uniquely human trait that fuels innovation, problem-solving, and artistic expression. It's the spark that ignites new ideas and propels us forward into uncharted territories. In this chapter, we will explore the fascinating world of creativity, delving into the psychology behind it, strategies to nurture your creative abilities, and how to apply creativity in various aspects of life.

The Essence of Creativity

Creativity is not confined to the realm of art and design. It permeates every facet of human existence, from scientific breakthroughs to entrepreneurial endeavors and everyday problem-solving. Here's why creativity is a vital asset:

1. Problem-Solving

Creative thinking enables us to approach problems from new angles, often leading to innovative solutions.

2. Adaptation

In a rapidly changing world, creativity is a valuable tool for adapting to new circumstances and seizing opportunities.

3. Self-Expression

Creativity provides an outlet for self-expression and a means of communicating ideas, emotions, and perspectives.

4. Inspiration

Creative individuals inspire others and foster a culture of innovation, driving progress in various fields.

The Psychology of Creativity

Understanding the psychological mechanisms of creativity can demystify the creative process and help you harness its power. Here are some key psychological aspects of creativity:

1. Divergent Thinking

Creativity often involves divergent thinking, which is the ability to generate a wide range of ideas and solutions.

2. Combining Ideas

Creative thinkers excel at combining seemingly unrelated concepts and ideas to produce novel outcomes.

3. Risk-Taking

Creativity often requires taking risks and venturing into the unknown, as well as the willingness to fail and learn from it.

4. Flow State

Many creative individuals experience a flow state, where they are fully immersed in their work, losing track of time and self-doubt.

Strategies for Nurturing Creativity

Creativity is a skill that can be cultivated and enhanced. Here are strategies to nurture your creative abilities:

1. Embrace Curiosity

Stay curious and open-minded. Ask questions, explore new interests, and seek out diverse experiences.

2. Cultivate a Creative Environment

Create a space that fosters creativity, whether it's a dedicated studio, a quiet corner, or a digital workspace.

3. Collaborate and Brainstorm

Engage in collaborative brainstorming sessions. Other perspectives can spark new ideas and insights.

4. Break Routines

Routine can stifle creativity. Shake up your habits, try new things, and break away from your comfort zone.

5. Keep a Journal

Maintain a journal to jot down ideas, observations, and inspirations. Reviewing your notes can lead to fresh insights.

6. Practice Mindfulness

Mindfulness techniques can help you stay present, reducing anxiety and freeing your mind for creative thinking.

Creativity in Action

As you continue your journey toward success, remember that creativity is your compass for navigating the complexities of an ever-evolving world. It's the force that propels you to imagine new possibilities, question the status quo, and find innovative solutions to challenges.

CHAPTER 31: THE ART OF PERSUASION

Persuasion is a timeless skill that has played a pivotal role in shaping human history. It's the art of influencing others' thoughts, feelings, and actions through effective communication and reasoning. In this chapter, we'll explore the principles of persuasion, techniques to master this skill, and the ethical considerations that come with it.

The Power of Persuasion

Whether you're trying to sell a product, win an argument, or rally support for a cause, persuasion is the key to achieving your goals. Here's why persuasion is a valuable asset:

1. Influence

Persuasion allows you to influence decisions and opinions, making it a valuable tool in personal and professional settings.

2. Communication

Effective persuasion enhances your ability to communicate ideas clearly and convincingly, fostering understanding and agreement.

3. Negotiation

In negotiations, persuasion helps you secure favorable outcomes by swaying the opinions and preferences of others.

4. Leadership

Leaders who can persuade inspire confidence and motivate their teams to achieve remarkable results.

The Psychology of Persuasion

Understanding the psychology behind persuasion is essential for mastering this art. Several psychological principles are at play when you seek to persuade others:

1. Reciprocity

People tend to reciprocate favors and kindness. Offering something of value can encourage others to be more receptive to your message.

2. Social Proof

Human beings often look to the behavior of others for guidance. Demonstrating that others have already accepted your idea can be persuasive.

3. Authority

People tend to trust and follow those they perceive as experts or figures of authority. Establishing your expertise can boost your persuasive power.

4. Scarcity

Highlighting the scarcity or exclusivity of what you're offering can create a sense of urgency and increase its perceived value.

Techniques of Persuasion

Mastering persuasion involves applying various techniques strategically. Here are some powerful persuasion techniques to consider:

1. Storytelling

Craft compelling stories that engage emotions and illustrate your point. Stories are memorable and relatable, making them effective persuasion tools.

2. Framing

Presenting information in a particular context or frame can influence how it's perceived. Use framing to highlight the benefits of your proposition.

3. Active Listening

Understanding your audience's needs and concerns is crucial. Active listening helps you tailor your message to their perspective.

4. Consistency

Encourage small commitments that align with your desired outcome. People tend to be consistent with their past behaviors and commitments.

Ethical Considerations

While persuasion is a powerful tool, it comes with ethical responsibilities. Always consider the ethical implications of your persuasive efforts. Here are some ethical guidelines to follow:

1. Transparency

Be transparent about your intentions and avoid deceptive tactics.

2. Respect

Respect others' autonomy and choices. Avoid manipulation or coercion.

3. Honesty

Present accurate information and avoid exaggeration or falsehoods.

4. Empathy

Consider the needs and perspectives of your audience. Ethical persuasion seeks a mutual benefit.

Persuasion in Practice

As you continue your journey toward success, remember that persuasion is a skill that can be honed over time. It's a tool for building connections, solving problems, and inspiring positive change. By mastering the art of persuasion, you can navigate complex social dynamics and guide others toward shared objectives.

CHAPTER 32: THE ART OF STORYTELLING

Storytelling is an ancient and universal human tradition, one that has been an essential part of our culture for millennia. Stories captivate our imaginations, transmit knowledge, and connect us on a deep level. In this chapter, we delve into the art of storytelling, exploring its profound impact on communication, its role in conveying complex ideas, and how you can harness its power to engage and persuade.

The Significance of Storytelling

Stories have been a fundamental part of human existence, transcending generations and cultures. Here's why storytelling is a vital skill:

1. Connection

Stories foster connection by eliciting empathy and allowing audiences to relate to characters and situations.

2. Memory

We remember stories far better than we do facts and statistics. A well-told story can make complex information more accessible and memorable.

3. Engagement

Stories are inherently engaging. They draw audiences in, making them active participants in the narrative.

4. Persuasion

Stories are persuasive tools. They can illustrate a point, inspire action, and change minds more effectively than a straightforward argument.

The Elements of a Good Story

A compelling story is more than a sequence of events. It involves several key elements:

1. Characters

Relatable and well-developed characters are at the heart of any good story. They drive the plot and engage the audience emotionally.

2. Conflict

Conflict is essential to storytelling. It creates tension, propels the narrative forward, and provides opportunities for character growth.

3. Setting

The setting establishes the context and atmosphere of the story. It helps the audience visualize and immerse themselves in the narrative.

4. Plot

The plot is the sequence of events that make up the story. It should have a clear beginning, middle, and end, with rising action, a climax, and a resolution.

5. Theme

A theme is the central idea or message of the story. It gives the narrative depth and purpose.

The Power of Emotion

Emotion is a driving force in storytelling. Engaging stories evoke emotions in the audience, creating a memorable and impactful experience. Here's how to harness the power of emotion in your storytelling:

1. Empathy

Create characters and situations that elicit empathy from your audience. When readers or listeners care about the characters, they become emotionally invested in the story.

2. Conflict Resolution

Conflict in a story can mirror real-life challenges. The resolution of conflict can provide hope and inspiration.

3. Emotional Arc

Characters should experience emotional growth or change throughout the story. This arc adds depth and resonance to the narrative.

Using Storytelling in Various Contexts

Storytelling is a versatile tool that can be applied in many aspects of life:

1. Marketing

Businesses use storytelling to connect with customers, making their products or services relatable and appealing.

2. Education

Educators use storytelling to make lessons more engaging and memorable.

3. Leadership

Leaders use storytelling to inspire and motivate their teams, sharing their vision and values.

4. Advocacy

Advocates use stories to raise awareness and create empathy for social and environmental causes.

The Journey Continues

Storytelling is a dynamic and evolving art. As you continue your journey, remember that the stories you tell, whether in business, education, or personal life, have the power to captivate, persuade, and inspire. By mastering the art of storytelling, you can craft narratives that resonate with others and drive positive change.

CHAPTER 33: THE SCIENCE OF DECISION-MAKING

Decision-making is an intrinsic part of human existence. We make choices every day, from the mundane to the life-altering. This chapter explores the fascinating world of decision-making, delving into the psychology, biases, and strategies that influence the way we make decisions. Understanding these aspects can empower you to make better choices in various aspects of life.

The Complexity of Decision-Making

Decision-making isn't always straightforward. It's influenced by a multitude of factors, including our emotions, values, beliefs, and the information available to us. Let's explore the complexities of this essential cognitive process:

1. Rational vs. Emotional

Decision-making often involves a balance between rationality and emotion. While some decisions are driven by logic and analysis, emotions can heavily influence others.

2. Heuristics and Biases

Our brains often use shortcuts, known as heuristics, to make decisions more efficiently. However, these mental shortcuts can lead to biases that affect the quality of our choices.

3. Risk and Uncertainty

Some decisions involve assessing and taking risks. Understanding risk tolerance and managing uncertainty is crucial for effective decision-making.

4. Group Dynamics

In social contexts, decisions are often made collectively. Group dynamics, such as conformity and peer pressure, can influence individual choices.

The Role of Cognitive Biases

Cognitive biases are systematic patterns of deviation from norm or rationality in judgment, often a result of the brain's attempt to simplify information processing. Here are some common biases that can impact decision-making:

1. Confirmation Bias

People tend to seek out information that confirms their existing beliefs and ignore contradictory evidence.

2. Anchoring Bias

This bias occurs when individuals rely too heavily on the first piece of information encountered when making decisions.

3. Availability Heuristic

We tend to overestimate the importance of information readily available to us, such as recent news or personal experiences.

4. Overconfidence Bias

Many individuals believe they are more skilled or knowledgeable than they actually are, leading to overconfident decision-making.

Strategies for Better Decision-Making

Despite the challenges and biases that can cloud our judgment, there are strategies and approaches that can lead to more effective decision-making:

1. Gather Information

Make an effort to collect relevant data and consider multiple perspectives before making a decision.

2. Delay Decisions

For complex or emotionally charged decisions, it can be beneficial to delay making a choice to allow time for reflection.

3. Consider Consequences

Think about the potential consequences of your decisions, both short-term and long-term.

4. Seek Feedback

Consult with others, especially those with expertise in the matter, to gain valuable insights.

5. Embrace Failure

Accept that not all decisions will lead to favorable outcomes. Learn from your mistakes and use them as opportunities for growth.

The Future of Decision-Making

The field of decision science continues to evolve, aided by advancements in technology and our understanding of human psychology. In an increasingly complex world, the ability to make sound decisions is a valuable skill.

CHAPTER 34: THE ART OF PERSUASION: INFLUENCING MINDS AND DECISIONS

Persuasion is a subtle yet powerful force that we encounter daily. From advertisements enticing us to purchase products to political speeches swaying our opinions, the art of persuasion surrounds us. This chapter delves into the intriguing world of persuasion, exploring its psychology, techniques, and ethical considerations.

The Psychology of Persuasion

Understanding how persuasion works begins with grasping the psychological underpinnings that drive it. Several key principles and concepts shed light on this:

1. The Principle of Reciprocity

People tend to feel obligated to reciprocate when someone does something for them. This principle forms the basis of many persuasion techniques.

2. Social Proof

We are often influenced by the actions and opinions of others. If many people are doing or believing something, it must be right, or so the logic goes.

3. Authority

Humans have a tendency to follow and trust authority figures. This is why endorsements by experts, doctors, or celebrities can be so persuasive.

4. Liking

People are more likely to be persuaded by those they like. Building rapport and establishing common ground can enhance the effectiveness of persuasion.

5. Scarcity

The fear of missing out on something valuable is a powerful motivator. Limited-time offers and exclusive deals leverage the scarcity principle.

Techniques of Persuasion

Persuasion techniques are used in various contexts, from marketing to negotiation. Here are some common methods employed to influence decisions:

1. The Art of Storytelling

Stories are a powerful way to engage emotions and convey messages. They create relatable scenarios that resonate with people.

2. The Use of Cognitive Dissonance

When people experience conflicting beliefs or actions, they tend to seek consistency. Persuasion can be achieved by highlighting this inconsistency.

3. The Foot-in-the-Door Technique

This strategy involves starting with a small request or commitment and then escalating to a larger one. Once someone agrees to the initial request, they are more likely to agree to a follow-up.

4. Nudging

Nudging involves making subtle changes to the way choices are presented to guide people toward a particular decision while preserving their freedom of choice.

Ethical Considerations

While persuasion can be a valuable tool for communication and advocacy, it also raises important ethical questions. Manipulative or deceptive persuasion techniques can harm individuals and society as a whole. It's crucial to consider the ethics of persuasion and use it responsibly.

The Dark Side of Persuasion

The world of persuasion has a shadowy side. Techniques employed unethically can exploit vulnerabilities and manipulate individuals. Recognizing these dark tactics is essential for protecting oneself from undue influence.

1. Manipulative Marketing

Some advertisements use psychological tricks to persuade consumers into making purchases they don't need or can't afford.

2. Propaganda

Throughout history, propaganda has been used to manipulate public opinion, often with dire consequences.

3. Coercion and Manipulation

In personal relationships or professional settings, individuals can be coerced or manipulated into actions against their better judgment.

Balancing Persuasion and Autonomy

In a world where persuasion is pervasive, striking a balance between influence and individual autonomy is essential. Empowering individuals to make informed decisions while recognizing the persuasive tactics aimed at them is a critical aspect of modern life.

CHAPTER 35: THE DIGITAL AGE: NAVIGATING THE INFORMATION REVOLUTION

Welcome to the digital age, a time of unprecedented technological advancements that have revolutionized the way we live, work, and connect with the world. In this chapter, we'll explore the profound impact of the digital revolution, from the rise of the internet to the challenges and opportunities it presents.

The Birth of the Internet

The internet, once a military and academic project, has become an integral part of modern life. It emerged from the ARPANET project in the late 1960s, connecting a handful of universities. Fast forward to today, where billions of people across the globe are connected.

The World Wide Web

The creation of the World Wide Web by Sir Tim Berners-Lee in 1991 transformed the internet from a text-based network into a multimedia platform. It's the web that brought us websites, hyperlinks, and the ability to share information in ways we now take for granted.

The Digital Divide

As the internet spreads, it has exposed a digital divide. While many enjoy the benefits of online access, there are still billions without reliable internet connections. Bridging this gap remains a critical challenge.

The Social Media Revolution

The rise of social media platforms like Facebook, Twitter, and Instagram has reshaped how we communicate and share information. It's not just about connecting with friends; it's about sharing news, shaping public opinion, and influencing the world.

Data, Privacy, and Surveillance

The digital age has raised concerns about data privacy and surveillance. Our online activities leave digital footprints that governments and corporations can track. It's a delicate balance between convenience and privacy.

E-commerce and the Sharing Economy

Online shopping and platforms like Airbnb have disrupted traditional industries. The convenience of e-commerce and the collaborative nature of the sharing economy have changed the way we consume goods and services.

The Gig Economy and Remote Work

Digital platforms have also given rise to the gig economy and remote work. People can now work from anywhere and choose jobs that suit their lifestyles.

Challenges of the Digital Age

As we embrace the digital age, we must also grapple with its challenges. These include cybersecurity threats, the spread of misinformation, and the potential for job displacement due to automation.

Digital Literacy and Critical Thinking

In this era of information overload, digital literacy and critical thinking are crucial. Being able to discern credible sources from misinformation is an essential skill.

The Future of the Digital Age

What does the future hold for the digital age? We can expect continued advancements in artificial intelligence, virtual reality, and the internet of things. These technologies will further shape our lives.

CHAPTER 36: THE POWER OF RENEWABLE ENERGY

In this chapter, we delve into one of the most critical topics of our time - renewable energy. As we continue our journey through the interconnected chapters of our world, understanding the transition to cleaner and more sustainable energy sources is paramount.

The Imperative of Renewable Energy

The 21st century has witnessed a growing global awareness of the environmental impact of fossil fuels, such as coal, oil, and natural gas. Climate change, air pollution, and resource depletion have forced us to reevaluate our energy choices. Renewable energy sources offer a way forward.

Solar Energy: Capturing the Sun's Power

Solar energy, harnessed through photovoltaic cells, has become a symbol of clean energy. Solar panels, made of semiconductor materials, convert sunlight into electricity. This technology has made solar energy accessible to homes and businesses worldwide.

Wind Energy: Harnessing the Earth's Breath

Wind turbines, with their elegant blades turning in the breeze, capture the kinetic energy of the wind and convert it into electricity. Wind farms have sprung up in various parts of the world, providing a substantial share of electricity generation.

Hydropower: Tapping into Nature's Flow

Hydropower, generated by the gravitational force of flowing water, has a long history dating back to ancient civilizations. Dams and hydroelectric plants now provide clean energy while also offering flood control and water storage.

Geothermal Energy: Earth's Inner Heat

Beneath the Earth's surface lies a vast reservoir of heat waiting to be tapped. Geothermal power plants extract this heat and convert it into electricity or direct heating for buildings. Iceland, for instance, relies heavily on geothermal energy.

Biomass Energy: Nature's Recycling

Biomass energy utilizes organic materials like wood, agricultural residues, and even algae to produce heat, electricity, and biofuels. It's a renewable energy source that recycles carbon, making it a sustainable option.

Challenges and Innovations

Transitioning to renewable energy is not without its challenges. Energy storage, grid integration, and intermittency issues need to be addressed. However, innovative technologies like advanced batteries, smart grids, and demand-side management are revolutionizing the energy landscape.

The Economic and Environmental Benefits

Investing in renewable energy offers economic advantages, such as job creation and energy independence. Moreover, it significantly reduces greenhouse gas emissions, mitigating the effects of climate change.

Global Efforts and Agreements

Nations around the world are committing to renewable energy targets and emissions reductions. International agreements like the Paris Agreement seek to unite countries in the fight against climate change.

The Path Forward

As we look to the future, the transition to renewable energy is a path of hope and necessity. It's a story of technological innovation, environmental stewardship, and the interconnectedness of our world. Each chapter in our energy history brings us closer to a sustainable future, and it's a journey we must continue to embrace.

CHAPTER 37: THE WONDERS OF DEEP SEA EXPLORATION

In this chapter, we embark on a journey to the depths of our planet's oceans, exploring the mysteries and marvels that lie beneath the surface. The oceans cover over 70% of the Earth's surface, yet we've only scratched the surface of what lies beneath.

The Abyssal Realm: A Hidden World

The ocean's depths, known as the abyssal zone, are a realm of darkness and crushing pressure. In the past, these depths were thought to be lifeless, but modern exploration has revealed a stunning diversity of life adapted to extreme conditions.

Submersibles and ROVs: Our Eyes in the Abyss

To explore the deep, scientists and adventurers rely on submersibles and remotely operated vehicles (ROVs). These high-tech vessels can withstand the immense pressure and darkness, allowing us to see and study deep-sea ecosystems.

Bioluminescence: Nature's Light Show

In the perpetual darkness of the deep, many creatures have evolved the ability to produce their own light through bioluminescence. From anglerfish to firefly squid, the deep-sea is illuminated by a stunning array of living light shows.

Extremophiles: Life Finds a Way

Extremophiles are organisms that thrive in extreme conditions, such as the hydrothermal vents on the ocean floor. These vents spew scalding, mineral-rich water, yet they are home to a vibrant ecosystem fueled by chemosynthesis.

Deep-Sea Discoveries: Titanic Wonders

Explorations have led to incredible discoveries, including the wreckage of the RMS Titanic. It's a somber reminder of the ocean's power and the tales it holds.

The Importance of Deep-Sea Research

Understanding the deep sea is vital for various reasons, from conserving biodiversity to discovering potential new medicines. It also helps us understand Earth's geology and climate history.

The Threats to the Deep Sea

Despite its remoteness, the deep sea faces threats from human activities like deep-sea mining, bottom trawling, and plastic pollution. Conservation efforts are crucial to protect these fragile ecosystems.

The Future of Deep-Sea Exploration

As technology advances, our ability to explore the deep sea grows. New missions to the ocean's depths, like the exploration of Europa, one of Jupiter's moons, provide a glimpse into the future of space and deep-sea exploration.

A Lasting Connection

Our exploration of the deep sea reminds us of the interconnectedness of our planet. The health of the oceans is vital to life on Earth, and the wonders we discover in the abyss serve as a testament to the resilience and adaptability of life on this planet. As we continue to explore and protect the deep sea, we unlock the secrets of our world's past and pave the way for a more sustainable future.

CHAPTER 38: THE ART AND SCIENCE OF BREWING COFFEE

In this chapter, we dive into the world of coffee, exploring the fascinating blend of art and science that goes into making a perfect cup of this beloved beverage. Coffee is not just a drink; it's a cultural phenomenon that has captivated the hearts and palates of people worldwide.

The Journey of a Coffee Bean

Our coffee journey begins in the lush coffee plantations of regions like Ethiopia, Colombia, and Brazil, where coffee beans are meticulously cultivated and harvested. The coffee bean's voyage from farm to cup is a testament to the dedication of farmers who nurture this precious crop.

The Roasting Process: Turning Green to Gold

Once harvested, coffee beans are subjected to the alchemical process of roasting. This critical step transforms green, unassuming beans into aromatic, flavorful gems. Roasters carefully control temperature and time to unlock the beans' unique flavors.

The Chemistry of Flavor: Notes and Aromas

Coffee's flavor complexity is astounding. We explore how chemical compounds like acids, sugars, and oils interact during brewing to create an intricate symphony of tastes and aromas, from fruity and floral to nutty and chocolatey.

Brewing Methods: Artistry Meets Science

From French press to espresso machines, the choice of brewing method significantly impacts the coffee's flavor. Each method requires precise measurements, water temperature, and extraction times to achieve the desired results.

The Perfect Cup: Precision and Craftsmanship

Crafting the perfect cup of coffee is a blend of precision and artistry. Baristas worldwide train tirelessly to master the art of pouring latte art, achieving that ideal crema on espresso, and balancing the brew's strength and flavor.

Coffee and Health: Fact and Fiction

We explore the science behind coffee's effects on health. From antioxidants to caffeine's impact on alertness, we separate myths from reality, helping readers make informed choices about their coffee consumption.

Coffee Cultures Around the World

Coffee is not just a drink; it's a cultural experience. We take a global tour of coffee cultures, from the Italian espresso bars to the Ethiopian coffee ceremonies, showcasing how coffee brings people together.

Sustainability and Ethical Sourcing

As coffee consumption grows, so do concerns about its environmental and ethical impact. We discuss sustainable farming practices, fair trade, and the efforts of the coffee industry to promote responsible sourcing.

The Future of Coffee: Innovation and Trends

The coffee industry is continually evolving. We delve into the latest trends, from cold brew to single-origin beans, and explore how technology and innovation are shaping the future of coffee.

A Shared Passion

Coffee unites people across continents, transcending language and borders. Whether sipped alone in quiet contemplation or shared over lively conversations, coffee is a reminder of our shared humanity and the simple joys that connect us all.

The Aroma of Tomorrow

Our exploration of coffee leaves us with a sense of wonder and appreciation for this remarkable beverage. As we continue to savor our daily brews, let's remember the countless hands and intricate processes that bring that comforting cup of coffee to our tables, and let's savor every sip with gratitude and curiosity.

CHAPTER 39: THE WONDERS OF EARTH'S OCEANS

In this chapter, we embark on a journey beneath the surface of our planet, exploring the awe-inspiring world of oceans. Earth's oceans cover more than 70% of its surface and are a testament to the remarkable diversity and beauty of life on our planet.

Unveiling the Depths

The ocean, with its vast and mysterious depths, has long captivated human curiosity. It's a place of extremes, with immense pressures, crushing darkness, and temperatures that range from freezing to scorching. Yet, even in these extreme conditions, life thrives.

Biodiversity Beyond Imagination

The ocean is home to an astonishing array of life forms, many of which remain undiscovered. From the tiniest plankton to the largest blue whales, the diversity of marine life is mind-boggling. We delve into the intricate food webs and ecosystems that sustain this rich biodiversity.

The Coral Reefs: Rainforests of the Sea

Coral reefs are some of the most vibrant and biologically diverse ecosystems on the planet. We explore how these undersea marvels form, their role in the marine ecosystem, and the threats they face, including climate change and coral bleaching.

The Ocean's Role in Climate Regulation

The ocean plays a crucial role in regulating Earth's climate. We discuss how oceans absorb and redistribute heat, influence weather patterns, and even act as carbon sinks, helping to mitigate climate change.

The Mysterious Deep Sea

The deep sea is one of the least explored and understood parts of our planet. We venture into the abyss to uncover the peculiar and often otherworldly creatures that inhabit this realm, from anglerfish with their glowing lures to the elusive giant squid.

Ocean Conservation and Preservation

Human activities, such as overfishing, pollution, and habitat destruction, threaten the health of our oceans. We examine the importance of marine conservation efforts and discuss how individuals and organizations are working to protect these precious ecosystems.

Oceans and Human Connection

Throughout history, oceans have played a crucial role in human exploration, trade, and culture. We explore how oceans have shaped human civilizations, influenced art and literature, and continue to provide inspiration to people around the world.

Challenges and Hope for the Future

While the challenges facing our oceans are significant, there is hope. We discuss innovative solutions, from sustainable fishing practices to marine protected areas, and the role each of us can play in preserving the oceans for future generations.

A Call to Action

In closing, we reflect on the interconnectedness of all life on

Earth and the responsibility we bear to protect our oceans. The wonders of the deep sea are a testament to the beauty and complexity of our planet, and it is up to us to ensure that these treasures endure for generations to come.

Exploring the Unknown

As we conclude our exploration of the oceans, let us remember that beneath the waves lies a world of wonder and mystery, waiting to be discovered. The oceans are a reminder of the boundless beauty and resilience of life on Earth, and it is our duty to be stewards of these remarkable ecosystems.

CHAPTER 40: THE ENIGMATIC WORLD OF UNDERGROUND CAVES

In this chapter, we venture deep into the Earth's crust to explore the hidden and mysterious world of caves. These subterranean landscapes are shrouded in darkness and mystery, concealing a wealth of geological wonders and fascinating ecosystems.

The Formation of Caves

Caves are born from a slow and patient dance between water, rock, and time. We delve into the intricate processes that create these underground wonders, from the dissolution of limestone to the carving power of flowing water.

Speleothems: Nature's Sculptures

Within caves, we encounter an array of stunning formations known as speleothems. Stalactites hang from cave ceilings like icicles, while stalagmites rise from the cave floor. Columns, draperies, and flowstones adorn the underground chambers, each with a unique story of formation.

Cave Fauna: Masters of Adaptation

The depths of caves are not devoid of life; in fact, they host a peculiar cast of creatures adapted to complete darkness.

We shine a light on troglobites—organisms that have evolved specialized traits to thrive in this extreme environment—and explain how these species have adapted to the challenges of their subterranean homes.

The Mystique of Bioluminescence

Some cave dwellers emit their own light through bioluminescence. We explore this fascinating phenomenon and its purpose in the pitch-black realm of caves, from attracting prey to finding mates.

Cave Art and Human History

Throughout history, caves have held profound significance for humans. We journey through time to uncover the ancient cave art of our ancestors, found in places like the Lascaux Caves in France and Altamira Cave in Spain. These masterpieces offer a glimpse into prehistoric cultures and their spiritual connection to these underground spaces.

Cave Exploration and Scientific Discovery

Caving enthusiasts, or spelunkers, risk their safety to explore and map caves, revealing their hidden secrets. We recount the daring adventures of early cave explorers and how their discoveries have contributed to our understanding of Earth's geological history.

The Challenge of Cave Conservation

Human activities, such as pollution and vandalism, threaten the delicate ecosystems within caves. We discuss the importance of cave conservation efforts and the need to strike a balance between exploration and preservation.

Cave Diving: Navigating the Underworld's Rivers

Some caves are partially or entirely submerged, creating a unique and perilous environment for cave divers. We dive into the world of cave diving and the challenges faced by those who explore the underground rivers and passages.

The Mystery Continues

As we conclude our exploration of underground caves, we acknowledge that there are countless uncharted caves waiting to be discovered. These hidden realms offer a tantalizing glimpse into the Earth's geological history and the resilience of life in extreme environments. The allure of caves lies in their enigmatic darkness, and the more we explore, the more we realize how much remains hidden beneath the surface.

The Subterranean Legacy

Caves serve as a reminder of the profound connections between Earth's surface and its hidden depths. They are an integral part of our planet's story, and it is our responsibility to protect and preserve these fragile and wondrous environments for future generations of explorers and scientists.

CHAPTER 41: THE DANCE OF EARTH AND SKY: EXPLORING ATMOSPHERIC PHENOMENA

In this chapter, we embark on an awe-inspiring journey through the Earth's atmosphere, unraveling the captivating world of atmospheric phenomena that shape our planet's climate and weather.

The Atmosphere: Earth's Protective Blanket

Our adventure begins by delving into the composition of the Earth's atmosphere—a blend of gases that envelops our planet and plays a pivotal role in sustaining life. We explore how the atmosphere acts as a shield against harmful solar radiation and traps heat, creating the conditions necessary for life to flourish.

A Palette of Colors: The Sky Above Us

As we gaze upward, we're greeted by the ever-changing canvas of the sky. From vibrant sunsets to the deep blues of clear days, we unravel the science behind the colors of the sky and learn how atmospheric particles scatter sunlight to create these stunning displays.

The Celestial Light Show: Aurora Borealis and Aurora Australis

Our journey takes us to the polar regions, where nature's most mesmerizing light show unfolds. We unveil the secrets behind the ethereal Aurora Borealis (Northern Lights) and Aurora Australis (Southern Lights), phenomena that have captivated human imaginations for centuries.

Clouds: The Sky's Storytellers

Clouds are more than just fluffy shapes in the sky; they hold clues about upcoming weather patterns and reveal atmospheric dynamics. We decipher the language of clouds, from cumulus to cirrus, and understand how they form, their role in precipitation, and their influence on climate.

Rainbows: Arcs of Color and Myth

The appearance of a rainbow after a rain shower never ceases to amaze us. We unravel the physics behind this optical marvel, exploring how raindrops act as prisms and create the spectral arcs that have inspired countless legends and stories.

The Roaring Winds: Hurricanes, Tornadoes, and Cyclones

Our atmospheric journey takes us to the heart of some of nature's most powerful and destructive forces: hurricanes, tornadoes, and cyclones. We delve into their formation, characteristics, and the science of predicting and tracking these tempests.

Mirages and Optical Illusions: Tricks of the Light

The atmosphere can bend and refract light in unexpected ways, giving rise to mirages and optical illusions. We demystify these phenomena, from the mirages in the desert to the "green flash" at sunset.

The Ozone Layer: Guardian of Life

High above our heads, the ozone layer shields us from harmful ultraviolet (UV) radiation. We uncover the story of ozone depletion, the environmental impact of human-made chemicals, and the global efforts to protect this vital shield.

Climate Change: The Atmospheric Challenge

In the final part of our atmospheric journey, we confront the urgent issue of climate change. We discuss the role of greenhouse gases in trapping heat, the consequences of a warming planet, and the collective actions required to address this global challenge.

A Continual Dance

As we conclude this chapter, we recognize that the Earth's atmosphere is in constant motion, an intricate dance of gases, particles, and energy that sustains all life on our planet. Understanding the beauty and complexity of atmospheric phenomena is not only a testament to human curiosity but also a vital step in our stewardship of Earth's delicate balance. Our journey continues as we connect the threads of knowledge from previous chapters and look ahead to the wonders still awaiting us in the remaining chapters of our book.

CHAPTER 42: UNVEILING EARTH'S HIDDEN WONDERS: THE MYSTERIES OF CAVES AND UNDERGROUND WORLDS

In this chapter, we embark on a thrilling expedition into the depths of the Earth, exploring the enigmatic and otherworldly landscapes found within caves and underground realms.

The Subterranean Frontier: A World Unseen

Our journey begins by peering into the entrance of a cave, a portal to a realm that often remains hidden from the surface world. We discuss the fundamental characteristics of caves and delve into the geological processes responsible for their formation.

Speleology: The Science of Caves

As we venture deeper into the darkness, we encounter the fascinating field of speleology—the study of caves. We explore the work of speleologists, scientists who unlock the secrets of caves by investigating their unique ecosystems, formations, and histories.

Stalactites and Stalagmites: Nature's Sculptors

One of the most captivating features within caves is the formation of stalactites and stalagmites. We reveal the geological processes that give rise to these intricate mineral sculptures and discuss the timescales involved in their creation.

Bioluminescent Marvels: Glow-in-the-Dark Creatures

Our journey takes a luminous turn as we uncover the enchanting world of bioluminescent organisms that thrive in the eternal darkness of caves. From glowworms to fungi, we delve into the science behind their magical illumination.

Subterranean Oases: Hidden Lakes and Rivers

Caves often hold hidden lakes and underground rivers, forming unique ecosystems. We explore the life that thrives in these subterranean oases and discuss their ecological significance.

Cave Art: Ancient Testaments to Human History

Deep within some caves, we find a treasure trove of prehistoric art, created by our ancestors thousands of years ago. We discuss the significance of cave art, the techniques used, and the stories these ancient paintings and engravings tell.

Cave Exploration: Daring Adventures

Our journey wouldn't be complete without a glimpse into the world of cave exploration. We learn about the intrepid cavers who risk their lives to unravel the secrets of Earth's underground realms, navigating through intricate mazes of passages and chambers.

The Cave Dwellers: Unique and Rare Species

Some caves are home to species found nowhere else on Earth. We explore the adaptations that allow these creatures to thrive in the challenging cave environment and the importance of cave conservation.

Underground Mysteries: Unearthed Treasures and Ancient Relics

Throughout history, caves have served as natural repositories for human history and geological wonders. We uncover the treasures and fossils that have been discovered in caves, shedding light on Earth's past.

Cave Preservation: Guardians of Subterranean Heritage

In the final part of our underground journey, we discuss the importance of cave conservation and the efforts made to protect these fragile and remarkable ecosystems for future generations.

A Subterranean Odyssey

As we conclude this chapter, we reflect on the awe-inspiring journey we've taken through Earth's hidden wonders. From the depths of caves to the heights of the atmosphere, our exploration of the natural world continues to unveil the mysteries and marvels of our planet. Our next chapter will carry us further along this extraordinary path, connecting the threads of knowledge from past chapters to the wonders that lie ahead.

CHAPTER 43: THE MARVELOUS WORLD OF BIRDS: FEATHERED WONDERS AND AVIAN BEHAVIORS

In this chapter, we take flight into the captivating realm of birds, exploring the diverse species, incredible adaptations, and fascinating behaviors that make them some of Earth's most enchanting creatures.

Feathers: Nature's Masterpiece

Our journey begins with the intricate world of feathers, the defining feature of birds. We delve into the structure and functions of feathers, from insulation to aerodynamics, highlighting the incredible engineering behind these lightweight wonders.

The Avian Family Tree: A Tapestry of Diversity

Birds come in an astonishing array of shapes, sizes, and colors. We navigate through the branches of the avian family tree, uncovering the myriad species that inhabit our planet, from the tiny hummingbird to the mighty condor.

Migration Marvels: Epic Journeys Across Continents

Migration is one of the most remarkable phenomena in the bird world. We explore the awe-inspiring journeys undertaken by migratory birds, spanning thousands of miles and involving astonishing feats of navigation and endurance.

Birdsong: The Language of the Skies

Birdsong is a universal language, and each species has its unique dialect. We listen to the melodies of birds and dive into the science of avian vocalizations, exploring their role in communication, territory defense, and courtship.

Nesting Instincts: Architectural Feats of Precision

Birds are nature's architects, crafting intricate nests that suit their specific needs. We examine the astonishing diversity of nest designs, from the hanging nests of oropendolas to the underground chambers of burrowing owls.

Courtship Displays: Love in the Avian World

Birds engage in elaborate courtship rituals to attract mates. We witness the extravagant displays of peacocks, the acrobatic flights of frigatebirds, and the mesmerizing dances of cranes, exploring the role of courtship in ensuring species survival.

Egg-cellent Engineering: The Miraculous Egg

Bird eggs are marvels of nature, offering protection and nourishment to developing embryos. We discuss the diverse shapes, sizes, and colors of eggs and the unique adaptations that allow them to thrive in various environments.

Avian Intelligence: Problem-Solving and Tool Use

Birds are far from simple creatures; many exhibit remarkable intelligence. We delve into the world of avian cognition, showcasing instances of problem-solving, tool use, and complex behaviors observed in species like crows and parrots.

Conservation Challenges: Protecting Our Feathered Friends

The world of birds faces numerous threats, from habitat loss to climate change. We explore the conservation efforts undertaken to protect these remarkable creatures and the importance of preserving biodiversity.

Human-Bird Connections: Birds in Culture and Science

Birds have profoundly influenced human culture and science throughout history. We trace the role of birds in mythology, art, and science, highlighting their significance in shaping our understanding of the natural world.

Birdwatching: A Passion for Feathers

Birdwatching is a beloved pastime for many, offering a profound connection to nature. We meet avid birdwatchers, or "birders," and learn about the joys and challenges of observing birds in the wild.

A Symphony of Life: Birds in Ecosystems

Birds play crucial roles in ecosystems as pollinators, seed dispersers, and predators. We explore the interconnectedness of bird species with their environments, emphasizing the delicate balance of life in which they participate.

A Feathered Finale

As we conclude our exploration of the avian world, we reflect on the diverse, enchanting, and sometimes bewildering nature of birds. From the smallest warbler to the largest albatross, they continue to inspire wonder and awe. Our journey through the natural world has been an incredible voyage of discovery, and the chapters that follow will weave together the tapestry of life on Earth, connecting us to the intricate web of existence that surrounds us.

CHAPTER 44: BENEATH THE SURFACE: THE ENIGMATIC WORLD OF MARINE LIFE

In this chapter, we plunge into the depths of our oceans, unveiling the mysteries of marine life that make up Earth's largest and least-explored biome. From the tiniest plankton to the colossal whales, the ocean teems with an astonishing diversity of life.

Oceans: Earth's Aquatic Giants

Our journey begins with an introduction to Earth's oceans, covering their vastness, interconnectedness, and the crucial role they play in regulating our climate and supporting life on our planet.

Ocean Zones: Layers of Life

The ocean is divided into distinct zones, each with its unique inhabitants and conditions. We explore the sunlit euphotic zone, the twilight zone, and the dark, frigid depths of the midnight zone, revealing the incredible adaptations of creatures to these environments.

Plankton: The Drifters of the Sea

Plankton may be small, but they are the foundation of ocean food webs. We dive into the world of phytoplankton and zooplankton, exploring their role as primary producers and the base of marine ecosystems.

Coral Reefs: Underwater Cities of Biodiversity

Coral reefs are among the most biodiverse ecosystems on Earth. We examine the intricate lives of corals, their symbiotic relationships with algae, and the multitude of species that call these vibrant underwater cities home.

The Mysterious Deep: Life in Abyssal Plains

The deep sea is a realm of extreme conditions, where life thrives despite darkness and crushing pressures. We meet bizarre creatures like anglerfish, giant squids, and dumbo octopuses, discovering how they've adapted to this harsh environment.

Kelp Forests: Underwater Forests of the Coast

Kelp forests are the coastal counterparts to coral reefs, offering habitat and sustenance to a wide range of species. We explore the unique biology of kelp and the intricate relationships between the inhabitants of these underwater forests.

Marine Migrations: The Great Ocean Wanderers

Just as on land, marine animals undertake epic migrations. We follow the incredible journeys of sea turtles, salmon, and humpback whales, uncovering the challenges and mysteries of these migrations.

Whales: Giants of the Deep

Whales are among the most majestic and enigmatic creatures in the ocean. We delve into their complex social structures, communication, and the role they play in nutrient cycling as

Earth's largest mammals.

Sharks: Predators and Guardians of the Sea

Sharks have ruled the oceans for millions of years. We explore their extraordinary adaptations as apex predators and their importance in maintaining the health of marine ecosystems.

Human Impact: The Plight of Our Oceans

Our oceans face numerous threats, from overfishing to plastic pollution and climate change. We discuss the human impact on marine life and the urgent need for conservation efforts to protect these fragile ecosystems.

Marine Sanctuaries: Hope for the Ocean

Conservationists and scientists are working tirelessly to safeguard marine life. We highlight the importance of marine sanctuaries and the remarkable recoveries seen in protected areas.

Ocean Exploration: Mapping the Unknown

The deep sea remains one of the least explored regions on Earth. We delve into the technology and methods used for ocean exploration, including remotely operated vehicles (ROVs) and submersibles.

A Call to Action: Preserving Our Oceans

As we conclude our journey through the depths, we reflect on the interconnectedness of all life on Earth and the vital role oceans play in sustaining life. We call for collective action to protect and conserve our oceans, ensuring they remain a source of wonder and life for generations to come.

Connected Realms: The Web of Life

Throughout this book, we've embarked on a voyage of discovery, from the heights of mountains to the depths of oceans. In the chapters that follow, we'll continue to explore the intricate connections that bind all living things on our planet, weaving together the stories of life in its myriad forms.

CHAPTER 45: THE SYMPHONY OF EARTH: BIODIVERSITY AND ECOSYSTEMS

In this chapter, we delve deeper into the intricate tapestry of life on Earth, exploring the astonishing diversity of species and ecosystems that make our planet a vibrant and interconnected biosphere.

Biodiversity: Nature's Masterpiece

Biodiversity is the cornerstone of life on Earth. We begin by defining biodiversity and its various components, from genetic diversity within species to the richness of ecosystems.

Species Richness: The Variety of Life

Our planet hosts an estimated 8.7 million species, though many remain undiscovered. We explore the fascinating world of species, their classification, and the factors that drive speciation.

Ecosystems: Nature's Communities

Ecosystems are dynamic communities of organisms and their physical environments. We journey through diverse ecosystems, from lush rainforests to arid deserts, explaining their unique characteristics.

Food Webs: Nature's Dinner Table

Food webs intricately link species within ecosystems. We dissect the roles of producers, consumers, and decomposers, illustrating the importance of each in maintaining ecosystem stability.

Keystone Species: Nature's Architects

Certain species play a disproportionate role in shaping ecosystems. We uncover the concept of keystone species and how their presence or absence can dramatically impact entire ecosystems.

Biodiversity Hotspots: Fragile Treasures

Earth's biodiversity is not evenly distributed. We spotlight biodiversity hotspots, regions of exceptional species richness, and the urgent need for their conservation.

The Importance of Biodiversity: Ecosystem Services

Biodiversity provides us with invaluable services, from pollination of crops to clean water. We explore the ecosystem services humans depend on and the economic value of biodiversity.

Threats to Biodiversity: The Human Footprint

Human activities pose significant threats to biodiversity, including habitat loss, pollution, invasive species, and overexploitation. We examine the root causes of these threats.

Conservation Strategies: Preserving Our Natural Heritage

Conservation efforts are vital for safeguarding biodiversity. We detail various conservation strategies, from protected areas and captive breeding programs to community-based conservation.

Success Stories: Triumphs of Conservation

Conservation efforts have yielded remarkable successes. We celebrate stories of species recovery, such as the California condor and the black-footed ferret, demonstrating that conservation works.

The Future of Biodiversity: Our Shared Responsibility

As we conclude this chapter, we emphasize the importance of global cooperation in conserving biodiversity. We explore emerging challenges, such as climate change, and how they intersect with biodiversity conservation.

The Circle of Life: Interconnected Chapters

Throughout this book, we've embarked on an incredible journey, unraveling the threads that connect all life on Earth. In the chapters that follow, we'll continue to explore the intricate web of life, linking the stories of species and ecosystems as we unravel the secrets of our planet's natural wonders.

CHAPTER 46: THE DANCE OF CLIMATE AND LIFE: A SYMBIOTIC RELATIONSHIP

In this chapter, we unravel the intricate dance between climate and life on Earth, exploring how living organisms influence the climate and, in turn, how climate shapes the world's ecosystems.

Earth's Climate: A Symphony of Forces

Our planet's climate is a complex interplay of various factors, from solar radiation and atmospheric composition to ocean currents and geological processes. We delve into these components, highlighting their roles in shaping climate patterns.

The Greening of Earth: Photosynthesis and Carbon Cycles

Photosynthesis, the miraculous process by which plants and other photosynthetic organisms convert sunlight into energy, plays a pivotal role in regulating Earth's climate. We explain how this process impacts carbon cycles and mitigates greenhouse gas concentrations.

Carbon Storage: The Lungs of the Planet

Forests, wetlands, and oceans act as vital carbon sinks, absorbing and storing vast amounts of carbon dioxide. We discuss the importance of these ecosystems in mitigating climate change and the threats they face.

Climate Adaptations: Nature's Survival Strategies

Life on Earth has adapted to various climate zones, from the scorching Sahara Desert to the icy tundra. We explore remarkable adaptations that enable species to thrive in extreme conditions.

Climate Extremes: The Challenge of Survival

Climate extremes, such as droughts and heatwaves, pose significant challenges to ecosystems and species. We examine how organisms cope with these events and the ecological consequences of extreme weather.

Biodiversity and Resilience: The Insurance Policy

Biodiversity enhances ecosystem resilience in the face of climate change. We showcase examples of diverse ecosystems that exhibit greater resistance and recovery from environmental disturbances.

Climate Change Impacts: A Global Wake-Up Call

Human-induced climate change is affecting ecosystems worldwide. We detail the impacts of rising temperatures, altered precipitation patterns, and sea-level rise on ecosystems and species.

The Role of Conservation: Protecting Ecosystems in a Changing Climate

Conservation is crucial in preserving biodiversity and mitigating climate change. We explore strategies that integrate conservation and climate adaptation, from creating corridors for species movement to restoring degraded ecosystems.

Restoring Balance: Human Responsibility in the Climate-Ecology Nexus

As stewards of the Earth, we hold the power to mitigate climate change and protect biodiversity. We discuss individual and collective actions that can help restore balance in the intricate relationship between climate and life.

A Planet in Flux: A Prelude to What Lies Ahead

As we conclude this chapter, we reflect on the dynamic nature of our planet's climate and ecosystems. We recognize the challenges and opportunities that lie ahead in our quest to safeguard the harmony between climate and life on Earth.

A Continuation of the Symphony: Harmonizing with Nature

Throughout this book, we've unveiled the interconnected stories of Earth's diverse life forms, ecosystems, and the forces that shape our world. In the chapters to come, we'll continue our exploration, weaving together the narratives of our planet's natural wonders, uncovering the mysteries of the cosmos, and understanding our place in the grand tapestry of existence.

CHAPTER 47: THE COSMIC ODYSSEY: UNVEILING THE MYSTERIES OF OUR UNIVERSE

In this chapter, we embark on a journey through the cosmos, unraveling the vastness of space, the birth and death of stars, and the enigmatic forces that shape the universe.

The Universe: A Cosmic Tapestry

The cosmos is a vast and intricate tapestry of galaxies, stars, planets, and cosmic phenomena. We begin by exploring the sheer scale of our universe, from the grandeur of galaxy clusters to the infinitesimal particles that make up all matter.

Stellar Life Cycles: Birth, Fusion, and Farewell

Stars are the celestial furnaces that produce light, heat, and the elements essential for life. We delve into the life cycles of stars, from their birth in stellar nurseries to the dramatic supernova explosions that disperse elements into space.

The Milky Way: Our Galactic Home

Our galaxy, the Milky Way, is a barred spiral galaxy containing billions of stars, including our Sun. We journey through its structure, understanding the dynamics that hold it together and the mysteries of the supermassive black hole at its center.

Exoplanets and the Search for Extraterrestrial Life

The discovery of exoplanets, worlds orbiting distant stars, has ignited our imagination about the potential for life beyond Earth. We discuss the methods used to detect exoplanets and the search for habitable environments and signs of extraterrestrial life.

Dark Matter and Dark Energy: The Cosmic Enigmas

Two elusive cosmic entities, dark matter and dark energy, make up the majority of the universe's mass-energy content. We explore their profound influence on the cosmos and the ongoing efforts to understand their nature.

The Expanding Universe: From the Big Bang to Cosmic Acceleration

The history of the universe is marked by its expansion, from the primordial singularity of the Big Bang to the accelerated expansion driven by dark energy. We trace this cosmic evolution and its implications for our cosmic fate.

Cosmic Time Travel: Wormholes, Black Holes, and Time Dilation

Concepts from theoretical physics, such as wormholes, black holes, and time dilation, challenge our understanding of space and time. We journey into the realms of these cosmic curiosities, exploring their effects on the fabric of the universe.

The Cosmic Microwave Background: A Glimpse of the Early Universe

The cosmic microwave background radiation provides a snapshot of the universe's infancy, just 380,000 years after the Big Bang. We delve into the significance of this relic radiation and its role in shaping the cosmos.

Cosmic Mysteries and the Future of Space Exploration

As we conclude this chapter, we reflect on the enduring mysteries of the universe and the prospects for future space exploration. From missions to study distant asteroids to the dream of human colonization on Mars, we contemplate the next steps in our cosmic odyssey.

A Continuation of Exploration: Navigating the Cosmos

Our exploration of the universe is an ongoing journey, a quest to unlock the secrets of the cosmos. In the chapters that follow, we'll continue our voyage, venturing deeper into the mysteries of space, time, and existence itself. As we continue our cosmic odyssey, we invite you to join us on this extraordinary adventure of discovery.

CHAPTER 48: THE OCEANS: EARTH'S DYNAMIC LIQUID REALM

In this chapter, we plunge into the depths of our planet's oceans, exploring their immense diversity, vital role in Earth's climate, and the ongoing scientific discoveries that reveal their mysteries.

The Blue Heart of Earth: Oceans Unveiled

Our Earth is often referred to as the "Blue Planet," and for good reason. Oceans cover over 70% of its surface, shaping its climate, geography, and providing habitat to a multitude of species. We begin our exploration by marveling at the vastness of the oceans, spanning the Pacific, Atlantic, Indian, Southern, and Arctic Oceans.

The Ocean Zones: Layers of Life and Complexity

The oceans are not uniform; they consist of various zones, each with its unique characteristics. From the sunlit euphotic zone, teeming with life, to the midnight abyssal plains where light never reaches, we dive into the layers that make up these aquatic realms.

Life in the Depths: Biodiversity Below the Surface

The oceans host a staggering array of life, from the microscopic plankton that forms the base of the marine food web to the apex predators like sharks and orcas. We explore the rich biodiversity of coral reefs, kelp forests, and hydrothermal vents that are hubs of life in the oceans.

The Ocean's Role in Climate Regulation

Oceans play a pivotal role in regulating Earth's climate. They absorb and store heat, influence weather patterns, and act as carbon sinks, mitigating the impacts of climate change. We investigate the complex mechanisms by which oceans influence climate on a global scale.

The Ocean Conveyor Belt: Thermohaline Circulation

One of the ocean's most critical functions is its involvement in the global conveyor belt, a system of currents that redistributes heat and nutrients around the world. We delve into the fascinating concept of thermohaline circulation and its significance in climate dynamics.

The Challenge of Ocean Exploration: Unveiling the Abyss

The ocean remains one of the least explored and understood parts of our planet. We discuss the technological innovations and challenges scientists face when studying the ocean's depths, from remotely operated vehicles (ROVs) to manned submersibles.

Marine Conservation: Protecting Our Ocean Heritage

Human activities, from overfishing to pollution, threaten the health of our oceans. We examine the importance of marine conservation efforts, including marine protected areas and sustainable fishing practices, in preserving the vitality of Earth's oceans.

Oceans and Human Civilization: Trade, Culture, and Inspiration

Throughout history, oceans have been vital to human civilization. They facilitated trade, shaped cultures, and inspired art and literature. We trace the historical relationship between humanity and the oceans, from ancient seafarers to the modern maritime world.

The Future of the Oceans: Challenges and Opportunities

In our concluding section, we assess the challenges facing our oceans, such as ocean acidification and plastic pollution, and the opportunities for sustainable management and conservation. We emphasize the crucial role of international collaboration in safeguarding the oceans for future generations.

Continuing the Journey: Exploring Earth's Wonders

Our exploration of the oceans is a testament to the boundless curiosity and determination of humanity. As we turn the page to the next chapter, we remain committed to uncovering the secrets of our planet and the cosmos beyond. Join us as we continue this extraordinary voyage through the interconnected wonders of Earth and the universe.

CHAPTER 49: THE FRAGILE SYMPHONY OF EARTH'S ATMOSPHERE

As we continue our journey through the interconnected wonders of our planet, we now turn our gaze skyward, exploring the complex and vital realm of Earth's atmosphere. From the air we breathe to the weather that shapes our daily lives, the atmosphere is a dynamic and fragile symphony that sustains all terrestrial life.

The Breath of Life: Composition and Layers of the Atmosphere

Our atmosphere is a delicate mixture of gases that provide the oxygen we breathe and the protective shield that absorbs harmful radiation from the sun. We dissect its composition and structure, from the troposphere where weather occurs to the exosphere that merges with outer space.

The Weather Makers: Understanding Atmospheric Phenomena

From gentle breezes to powerful storms, the atmosphere is a theater of ever-changing weather patterns. We explore the mechanisms behind weather phenomena, from the formation of clouds and rain to the development of hurricanes and tornadoes. Weather, with its beauty and ferocity, is a manifestation of the atmosphere's dynamic nature.

Climate Change: Unraveling the Human Influence

In recent decades, the Earth's climate has undergone significant changes due to human activities. We delve into the science of climate change, examining the role of greenhouse gases, the consequences of rising temperatures, and the urgent need for mitigation and adaptation strategies.

The Ozone Layer: Guardian of Life

High in the stratosphere, the ozone layer plays a crucial role in protecting life on Earth. We recount the discovery of the ozone hole, its link to human-made chemicals, and the global efforts that led to the Montreal Protocol—an inspiring example of international cooperation.

The Dance of Light: Aurora and Atmospheric Phenomena

The atmosphere is not just a stage for weather; it also showcases mesmerizing displays of light, such as the aurora borealis and aurora australis. We unveil the science behind these celestial ballets and explore other atmospheric wonders like halos, mirages, and noctilucent clouds.

Air Quality and Pollution: The Price of Progress

The air we breathe is not always pure. We confront the challenges of air pollution, discussing its sources, impacts on human health, and the measures taken to improve air quality. The battle for clean air is an ongoing endeavor.

Beyond Earth: The Atmospheres of Other Planets

Our exploration takes us beyond our home planet as we examine the diverse atmospheres of other celestial bodies, from the carbon dioxide-laden air of Venus to the thin, frigid envelope of Mars. Comparing these atmospheres offers valuable insights into the uniqueness of Earth.

The Future of Earth's Atmosphere: Our Responsibility

In our closing section, we reflect on the fragility of Earth's atmosphere and the collective responsibility we bear in preserving its integrity. Whether addressing climate change, air quality, or space exploration, the future of our atmosphere lies in our hands.

Continuing the Journey: Guardians of the Planet

As we turn our eyes back to Earth, we are reminded of the remarkable interconnectedness of our planet's systems. The atmosphere is not just above us but within us, a reminder that our actions reverberate through this fragile symphony of life. Join us in the next chapter as we delve into the final frontier, exploring the mysteries of the universe beyond our atmosphere.

CHAPTER 50: BEYOND OUR BLUE MARBLE: THE QUEST FOR COSMIC UNDERSTANDING

As we conclude this journey through the diverse wonders of our planet and the boundless reaches of our universe, we find ourselves on the cusp of an exciting frontier—the exploration of space. In this final chapter, we embark on a cosmic odyssey, delving into the mysteries of the cosmos beyond our atmosphere.

The Cosmic Perspective: Our Place in the Universe

Looking up at the night sky, we ponder our place in the vastness of the cosmos. From ancient stargazers to modern astronomers, humans have sought to understand the universe's origins, structure, and fate. We explore how our knowledge of the cosmos has evolved over the centuries.

Telescopes and Observatories: Windows to the Universe

The development of telescopes revolutionized our understanding of the universe. We journey through the history of these instruments, from Galileo's humble telescope to the cutting-edge observatories that peer deep into space, revealing distant galaxies, nebulae, and celestial phenomena.

Exploring the Solar System: Voyages to Our Cosmic Neighbors

Humans have sent robotic emissaries to explore our solar system, from the first moon landing to the exploration of distant planets like Mars and Saturn. We recount these missions, highlighting the discoveries that have reshaped our understanding of our celestial neighbors.

Life Beyond Earth: The Search for Extraterrestrial Intelligence

The question of whether life exists beyond Earth has captivated the human imagination. We delve into the scientific efforts to detect signs of life elsewhere in the universe, from the study of extremophiles on Earth to the search for exoplanets in habitable zones.

Cosmic Mysteries: Dark Matter and Dark Energy

The universe holds many enigmas, and two of the most perplexing are dark matter and dark energy. We unravel these cosmic mysteries, discussing their role in the universe's expansion and the ongoing scientific quest to understand their nature.

The Future of Space Exploration: Humans on Mars and Beyond

With plans to send humans to Mars and renewed interest in lunar exploration, the future of space exploration is promising. We look at the technologies and aspirations that drive these ambitious missions and the potential for humans to become a multi-planetary species.

Cosmic Phenomena: Supernovae, Black Holes, and Pulsars

Exploring the more extreme corners of the universe, we encounter supernovae, black holes, and pulsars. These cosmic phenomena, born from the fiery deaths of stars, challenge our understanding of the fundamental forces governing the cosmos.

The Cosmic Symphony: Gravitational Waves

In recent years, scientists have achieved a remarkable feat—the detection of gravitational waves. We discuss the significance of this breakthrough, its role in confirming Einstein's theory of relativity, and the fascinating celestial events that produce these ripples in spacetime.

The Ethical Frontier: Space Exploration and Human Responsibility

As we extend our reach into space, we must grapple with ethical questions. From planetary protection to responsible space mining, we examine the moral dilemmas and responsibilities that arise as we expand our presence in the cosmos.

The Continuation of Human Exploration: Uncharted Frontiers

Our cosmic journey comes to an end, but the exploration of space continues. We reflect on the enduring spirit of human curiosity and the uncharted frontiers that await future generations. The cosmos, with its infinite wonders, beckons us to explore, understand, and cherish our place within it.

Conclusion: A Journey of Discovery

In this final chapter, we have traversed the realms of our planet and ventured into the cosmos itself. From the smallest particles to the most distant galaxies, the universe is a tapestry of mysteries and marvels awaiting our exploration. As we conclude this 50-chapter journey, we are reminded that the pursuit of knowledge, curiosity, and the desire to understand our world and the universe are what define us as a species. Let our quest for discovery be a beacon guiding us to new horizons, forever connected to the vast and wondrous cosmos in which we live.

Printed in Great Britain
by Amazon